MUN-E:

How to be Social, Diplomatic, Win Allies, Influence People, & GAVEL!

Eugene Geis, Ph.D.
& Anthony White

Model UN Education
http://www.modeluneducation.com

Lightstream Enterprise LLC
911 Wellington Pl. Aberdeen, NJ 07747

ISBN: 978-0-9856486-1-9

First Official Paperback printing, October 2012

Model UN Education and Social Intelligence Education are being administered under Lightstream Enterprise LLC with all materials being handled under The MUNIVERSITY.

For information regarding special discounts for bulk purchases, please contact Model UN Education by email: bookorders@muneducation.com

Edited by Michael Rocco, Anthony White, & Eugene Geis
Cover design by Eugene Geis
Interior Illustrations by Tom White
Images licensed through iStockPhoto
Printed by 48HrBooks

Don't forget to visit us at
http://www.modeluneducation.com

Table of Contents

Introduction i

"A Moment of Clarity" xv

CHAPTER 1: The Mantra of MUN 1

    A BRIEF HISTORY OF THE UNITED NATIONS........................... 3

    STRUCTURE OF THE UNITED NATIONS 5

"The Picket Fence" 12

CHAPTER 2: The Attitude of Winning 13

    CONFIDENCE WITH CHARISMA 14

    THE GOAL OF ALL PERSONAL INTERACTIONS....................... 17

    THE GOAL ORIENTED MINDSET 18

    THE FINE BALANCE BETWEEN SELFISH AND SELFLESS.......... 21

    DRILLS.. 23

"The Family" 26

CHAPTER 3: Teflon Smooth 27

    BODY LANGUAGE.. 28

    VOCAL TECHNIQUES 30

    RAPPORT 34

    AWARENESS 38

    DRILLS.. 42

"All the World is a Stage" 46

CHAPTER 4: The Cast of Characters 47

    The Newbie 47

The "Absent Joe" 50

The International Delegate 51

The Veteran 54

The Gavel Hunter 55

The Activist 58

The Diplomat 60

"Deep Thoughts" 64

CHAPTER 5: Rhetoric and Dialectic 65

THEORY 67

EXAMPLES& DRILLS 72

Rhetoric and Dialectic in Committee 75

"Light Work" 82

CHAPTER 6: The Blueprint 83

STRATEGIES FOR INDIVIDUALS 84

STRATEGIES FOR TEAMS 93

ADVANCED PLAYMAKING 98

"Nice Kimono Dawg" 108

CHAPTER 7: Dressed for Success 109

WOMEN'S ATTIRE 111

MEN'S ATTIRE 115

THE FINER DETAILS: 118

"The Message" 120

CHAPTER 8: ExpositoryWriting 121

Essential Practices for MUN Writing 122

Position Papers 127

Working Papers and Resolutions 130

"Napoleon... duh!" 140

CHAPTER 9: The Art of Crisis 141

Creativity & Vision 148

Writing 149

Your Frame 151

"Dark Forces" 156

CHAPTER 10: The Dark Arts 157

A RECIPE FOR MADNESS 158

THE COOKBOOK 160

Advanced Rapport 169

"Not So Stick Anymore" 174

CHAPTER 11: Going Digital 175

The Internet Is The Future 175

Creating Your Wordpress Site 178

Plan your site for your MUN Club 188

General Web Strategy 190

APPENDIX A 191

Guide to Parliamentary Procedure 191

The Compendium of Common Motions 195

APPENDIX B 197

A Guide to Research 197

RESEARCH STEPS FOR PRESENT-DAY COMMITTEES 199

RESEARCH STEPS FOR HISTORICAL COMMITTEES 201

FREQUENTLY ASKED QUESTIONS ABOUT RESEARCH 203

APPENDIX C 207

A Guide to Club Management 207

GLOSSARY 217

REFERENCES 221

To those who've shown me how they lead by example...

E. Geis

A special thanks to Ronald Schuster... Your love of the Model United Nations made this book possible.

A. White

Introduction

Thus a deity hath spoken: Let there be the MUNiverse!

Welcome to the world of **MUN-E**, aka **Model UN Education**. We have a few quick rules that will help you learn our philosophy of **Success**. *Not just in Model UN*, but in **LIFE as a Whole**.

1. People need to <u>RESPECT</u> you before they will <u>listen</u> to you.
2. People need to <u>LIKE</u> you before they will <u>do</u> as you ask of them.
3. People need to <u>KNOW</u> that you have the respect and kindness to listen to them <u>BEFORE</u> they will **Like** and **Respect** you.

You may have heard this before and *you may even know it*... but **do you <u>practice</u> these things?**

There is a strange habit among the Model UN folks... The first lesson that most MUNers and their respective club advisors use is a formal debate within the historical context of current events and political feuds. While we *understand* this preference for tossing the delegate directly into the fire of political argument, we think that this method skips over **THE MOST IMPORTANT SKILLS**.

The 3 rules we've just given you comprise the basic formula of MUN-E (Model UN Education) and when you take these rules and include the skills we teach in this book, you **will become more confident, you will speak better, and debate will become a welcome challenge.**

This method has been proven over and over again. Prometheus discovered fire and we gave it to our delegates. Listen, we're not messing around. Our Model UN club only meets once a week for about one hour each meeting... and yet we have taken the Best Large Delegation crown multiple times in the nation's largest and most competitive conferences. Our school has maintained its reputation for more than 40 years. Our focus is not based on awards, but if the measure of skill is commensurate to awards, we're Top 5.

Do you want to know how we do it?

WE TEACH *SOCIAL INTELLIGENCE*

You can also call it "Human Engineering" if you want to be scientific about it...

But for the real scientist in you, we've made a graph titled:

THE AXIS OF EXCELLENCE

FEATURING: The Success Spectrum!!!

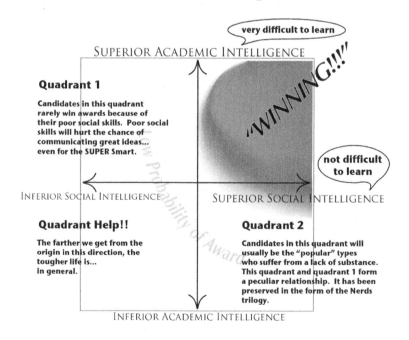

The *Success Spectrum* is the fountain from which all GAVELS spring. Use the brief descriptions above as an introduction to the raw power of Social Intelligence in the Model UNiverse. Please note that our axes are defined by "Social Intelligence" and "Academic Intelligence."

Let's take a look at Academic Intelligence first. Academic Intelligence is what people call "book smarts." You know the smartest kid in your math or science class? Well that kid is probably really good at doing her homework, understanding the teacher, and doing multiplication in her head. But is she *"cool?"* Academic Intelligence is not specific to any subject... it's pretty much what we all think of as "smart." We know you understand already that being "smart" may not win you as many friends as being "cool." And in Model UN, you need to have something we'll call *smart coolness*. This is called Social Intelligence.

Social intelligence is an entirely different beast than its academic brother. Our *Success Spectrum* is more heavily weighted by Social Intelligence because in the classroom, in business, in Model UN, and in life... Social Intelligence is a little more important than the other ones. This book starts with techniques for learning social intelligence. Take another look at our pretty little graph. At the lower left, there is no shade indicating a Low Probability of Award, i.e. low social intelligence and academic intelligence will make it very difficult to win at MUN. Towards the top right, as the gray fades in, increasing social intelligence results in a MUCH higher probability of winning awards! *Even if you have very* average *academic intelligence,* **social intelligence makes you a competitor**. Get ready for your first lesson in Social Intelligence!

Features of the Graph

We have separated the graph into four quadrants. Each quadrant represents a 'type' of Model UN delegate that can improve their performance in one way or another. We'll start with a description of the top left: Quadrant 1.

<u>Quadrant 1:</u> The reason it is labeled with a ONE is because the type of delegate who fits into this category is typically a loner. They do not spend a lot of time with other delegates and it is difficult for them to have a good, fun conversation. Speaking with these delegates isn't very easy. They don't seem like good leaders, and they are difficult to 'read.' The weird thing is that most of these delegates are academically intelligent, which means that *social skills can turn them into* **immediate** winners. These delegates have great potential to become true diplomats.

<u>Quadrant 2:</u> This quadrant is labeled TWO because these delegates are very effective when paired with delegates from different areas of the graph. Individually, they are poor Model UN delegates but they are excellent *social engineers*. Other delegates will describe them as dynamic, friendly, attractive, and persuasive. Unfortunately, they are usually low on substance.

If you are a part of Quadrant 2 please don't think that MUN is hopeless. On the contrary, MUN is a place where Superior Social Intelligence can disguise how little a delegate truly knows. The most socially intelligent delegates can be so "personable" and socially adept that they are able to convince an entire room to follow them. There are a multitude of "historical demagogues" you can research. Ronald Reagan is a great example.

On our Axis of Excellence, there is a little dark sliver of "winning-ness" that begins fading in along the line of Superior Social Intelligence. This is the proof that *CHARISMA (see Chapter 3.1)* can be *more* valuable than book smarts. There are countless studies on the income of business employees and how their salaries can be shown to reflect their height, attractiveness, and friendliness. People with these features can come off as "charismatic" but charisma is not only reserved for those individuals. **A strong understanding of charisma can help <u>anyone</u> succeed regardless of their appearance.**

NOTE on Q1 and Q2 – *a large number of delegates will think that they're in Quadrant 1 while they're actually in Quadrant 2. Similarly, there will also be delegates who think they're in Quadrant 2 but actually belong in Quadrant 1. Be honest with yourself. Regardless of where you think you are on our graph, this book will carry you in a Northeast direction... We will start walking you DIRECTLY towards Superior Social Intelligence and your own investigation of those techniques will carry you far up the Academic Intelligence axis, i.e. the "book-smarts" ladder.*

<u>Quadrant Help!!</u> If you're in this quadrant, we understand your dilemma. You're in dire straits but we can, at least, set you on the road to recovery.

1. You CAN and you WILL make yourself "smarter". It requires discipline and lots of reading to get informed so get ready. Believe us there is a lot to learn.

2. You need to get over any sort of shyness or embarrassment. You CAN and you WILL start

talking to "new" and "random" people. Social intelligence is a skill that you learn through experience. It is trial and error. Prepare yourself for the emotional journey that will follow as you learn these new skills.

WINNING!! This quadrant is your goal. By reading this far you have proven that you have the patience and enthusiasm which shows that you have above average Academic Intelligence *already*. This means **YOU CAN LEARN** Social Intelligence. Social Intelligence holds more influence on your success than Academic Intelligence!!!

A FEW SUBTLE FEATURES:

There's one more feature you should probably ask about our Success Spectrum. There is a mixed relationship being shown along the axis of "SUPERIOR ACADEMIC INTELLIGENCE." For the delegate who is *super*-smart, he or she will become **LESS** likely to win an award *if they do not show **better than average** Social Intelligence*! But look how quickly the (*high probability*) gray fully fades in as that delegate learns the techniques of social intelligence!

As advisors of a very successful MUN group, we are amused by the large number of delegates that concentrate purely on policy. Our students are always asking for better ways to research... And you're all *SO* obsessed with position papers. **BUT MOST OF YOU COMPLETELY OVERLOOK YOUR** *AVERAGE* **OR** *BELOW AVERAGE* **SOCIAL SKILLS!** And you don't even realize that social skills are actually *MORE* important than the academic substance in most situations and arguments!

THE MORAL OF THE STORY

This book is going to approach MUN skills from the angle of Social Intelligence. Each chapter will build you into a better and more effective interpersonal delegate. The more seriously you approach the exercises in this book, the more often you will notice that it is easier to speak to everyone else, too. Interviewing will become effortless, negotiating will become a smoother process, and arguing will not feel as stressful as before. Instead, you'll see all of these situations as opportunities to shine. In committee, order will be restored from chaos... and you will be the harbinger* of mutual prosperity. You will be seen as The Diplomat. You will command respect in a room of hundreds and the chairperson will see you as a contributor to the well-being of all sentient beings.

TABLE OF CONTENTS

There has been special care taken in the organization of the contents of this book. Realize that each chapter is developing a skill that lays the foundation for the next lesson to come.

CHAPTER 1: Mantra of MUN

The first chapter is a quick description of the logistical goals of Model UN; it is entitled the "Mantra." Most of you know these details already but for the noobs, aka "the newbies," the United Nations is an organization built upon an IDEAL (and a "mantra" is a repeated phrase

---

* If you notice words or phrases that you've never heard before, YOU SHOULD LOOK THEM UP! Aren't you reading this because you want to get better!? Smarter!? More successful!? ...well then start doing the work! Google the word 'harbinger' and challenge yourself to use it in a speech. From here on it's YOUR JOB to impress people.

that is to aid in meditation). In reality, the ultimate goals of the United Nations require profound belief and consistent focus upon the ideals of peace, welfare, and stability. No matter how you approach your role as a delegate, those core values must radiate from your presence and oration (even when you act evil). Just remember your mantra, your goal. Then hurry on to the next chapter to start chomping on the real meat of the most powerful MUN delegates.

CHAPTER 2: Attitude of Winning

This chapter begins your descent into the depths of social intelligence and the core qualities used to build a magnetic and effective character. Charisma, confidence, and their effects on personal interactions are demonstrated in this section. We also point out another crucial piece that ties these character traits into a true, effective leader: the ***goal-oriented mindset.***

No matter how ambitious you are, if you have no goals you have no path to success. If you're going to read further and you are really going to dedicate yourself to becoming an effective leader, you need to practice every day. Simple habits can make the difference. For example, you can get a small journal and start writing some goals for yourself. Start simple. Write a few changes that you hope this book will help you achieve.

CHAPTER 3: Teflon Smooth

"Teflon Smooth" is a metaphor for the really slick people that seem to always slip right below the radar. In other words, it refers to the delegates with Superior Social Intelligence. It sounds sneaky (and there's some truth to that observation) but it more closely resembles a set of traits that make someone "cool." Yes, there are traits; well-defined traits actually. This chapter defines the basic skills that you need to develop including body language, vocal techniques, and rapport. Your ability to master these three techniques and gauge your audience will catapult your effectiveness as a delegate. We can't stress this chapter enough.

CHAPTER 4: The Cast of Characters
Now that we've outlined the type of personality that you need to create for yourself, we're going to show you the types of personalities that you're going to encounter on your little adventure into the MUNiverse. The compendium included in this chapter provides brief character sketches of various delegates. Use this section as an opportunity to learn about your enemy. Remember the teachings of Master Sun Tzu, "Know your enemy and know yourself and you can fight a hundred battles without disaster."

CHAPTER 5: Rhetoric and Dialectic
Chapter 5 is a "How-To" for demonstrating superior powers of debate. It will carefully explain exactly how to take all of your newly improved social skills and apply them to the academic debates and negotiations that occupy the delegates of every MUN conference in existence. A quick explanation of the theory is followed by real-world examples. In the last section of the chapter, you practice.

CHAPTER 6: The Blueprint
The capping stone of chapters 3 thru 6 is this ultimate strategy guide for individual and double

delegations. This is the foundation of techniques that will help you develop the ability to "mastermind." There are also four strategies for your school if you're blessed with a very large MUN club. Put your multiple delegations to work for you and maximize the effectiveness of Luxembourg, the Democratic People's Republic of Korea, and Djibouti. Meaningless countries can become global voices in the affairs of the General Assemblies. We'll show you how to happily dismantle your enemies with sheer numbers and tactics. In the 1970's and 80's, our high school club was known to employ these types of strategies and won **multiple** "best large delegation" awards **each year.**

CHAPTER 7: Dressed for Success

Dress codes should not require very much detail. Although it might be better included as an appendix, we've included this as a chapter because it seems lost to some of the shameful characters that can sometimes be noticed at large conferences. This is the deal: you're technically post-adolescent. You should be able to dress yourself. You should be clean, odorless, and hygienic. You should be aware of your appearance. Unfortunately, some of these rules of conduct and appearance aren't as obvious to everyone as we'd love to think. Thus, we have the typical chapter on standard professional dress and hygiene policy.

CHAPTER 8: Expository Writing

Despite the fact that position papers can strongly influence a chair's opinion about you, your writing will only develop through practice. This chapter will give you a great deal of information about HOW writing is used in Model UN. The problem is that you need to do a lot of practice to get good at it. You need to start READING MORE BOOKS. Through reading and writing, you'll figure out how to write better. We're not going to fool you into believing that it's easy enough to learn in a single chapter of any book.

This chapter will describe the types of habits that will help you write convincing arguments. You'll also learn the expected format for position papers, working papers, and resolutions. Again, we understand your nervousness when it comes to authoring these "papers," but trust us – your fears are misplaced ...unless you don't know how to read and write. In that case, there's not much anyone will be able to do for you and we're not sure what you're doing with this book.

CHAPTER 9: The Art of Crisis

When delegates are ready to move beyond the comfort of large numbers and onto the echelon of elite decision makers, they enter the realm of Crisis. Crisis committees are whirlwinds of intensity and turmoil. The best delegates are deafening personalities. Every crisis is an adventure, the likes of which include plotlines influenced by spies, strategists, and turncoats. Policy sometimes takes a backseat to effectiveness and you must stand out or you'll get chewed up and spit out. We've watched it happen. It is extremely important for you to change your perspective when you move from large delegations to smaller crisis committees. This might be the only chapter of any book you'll ever read about crisis committees and we know it will blow your mind. You'll also understand why *The Dark Arts* follow...

CHAPTER 10: The Dark Arts

This chapter is a dark, circuitous path down the rabbit hole of social graces and 'business' acumen. Getting things done is not always so easy. Sometimes you have to shout louder than the next guy in order to be heard. Sometimes you have to step on someone's toes in order to get ahead in the crowd. This isn't a chapter about causing harm to anyone. Instead, this is a short recipe list of ways to get ahead.

The Dark Arts acknowledges that all is fair in love and war. Even in the MUNiverse negotiations can become a war for 'territory.' Regardless of how much territory you're willing to compromise, you must teach your opponents respect. If you truly want to be at the top of the mountain, it's easy to see that there's much less room at the top than there is at the bottom. It can be a treacherous path up that mountain... This chapter might even show you some shortcuts to avoid social hypothermia and political death.

CHAPTER 11: Going Digital

Want to manage your club and share articles and post topics and get your MUN-E Skillz rockin' in cyberspace? We know. This is a huge piece of the puzzle, nowadays, especially for club organization and conference advertising. So we're going to teach you how to make your own website and/or a website for your club. It is easy to manage, your posts will communicate with your Facebook group and Twitter followers and you can post links, pictures, articles, music, and or video with ease.

Don't lie, you're in love with this book. *Le sigh.*

THE APPENDICES
Parliamentary Procedure and Research

Yes, we KNOW that most of you are concerned about writing position papers and resolutions. You probably also think that you are weak at research too. Luckily we include HOW-TO guides to aid you in your struggle, but we're not going to overdo it here. These things are very, very systematic.

Parliamentary Procedure is a rulebook. You aren't allowed to change those rules. You must learn them, but you can also keep a list of those rules with you. Our first appendix contains these rules. We strongly encourage you to become familiar with them. You'll never know when you might need them.

Research is the subject of Appendix B. You should research efficiently and effectively. Research is probably the most important part of choosing a valid position when writing a position paper. A valid position is the best *thesis* for any position paper. When you learn the arts of Rhetoric and Dialectic from Chapter 5, you'll learn how to carve a deep stance and fortify your opinions with validity.

Our last Appendix is for advisors or students who want to understand how a successful Model UN club can be run. If you have a new advisor, you might want to share it with him/her.

So... Are you ready? Read Chapter 1 and start chanting your 'MANTRA'...

"A Moment of Clarity"
by Thomas White

CHAPTER 1: The Mantra of MUN

"Om Mani Padme, Munnnnnnnn"

DIPLOMACY IS OUR MANTRA! Say it loud and say it proud. If you are unfamiliar with what a mantra is or what diplomacy means, bow your head in shame. You have brought great dishonor! You may be forgiven but only if you will learn, young grasshopper. We will teach you your *mantra*—a meaningful phrase on which to place your concentration. And you will learn that your mantra is none other than **DIPLOMACY**.

Diplomacy is probably *the* most important word in Model UN. It is equivalent to the Japanese **"bushido"** as a code for life. Diplomacy allows you to be popular in committee. You are a leader yet you are open to suggestions. You have a commanding voice yet you are polite to all. You have independent ideas but you are willing to compromise for the greater good. When a true diplomat acts **and** listens, it is a representation of everything that is holy and cherished in the world of the United Nations.

Diplomacy is the foundation to the UN's system of **ideals** and it is important for you to understand how to demonstrate it. If you are lucky, the gods may smile upon you and offer a glimpse of the true mystical properties associated with diplomacy as well. Think of it like the *Force* from the Star Wars movies. It's in and around you at all times, at least in theory. It's your duty in life to master its energies.

Successful delegates understand the importance of diplomacy and use it early and often. The appearance of diplomacy is essential for success (Keyword: "appearance"). You need to use the word frequently in speeches. You need to attempt to broker compromise between delegations. You need to eat, live, and breathe diplomacy. Remember, it is your *mantra*. It needs to be so ever present in your mind that if you have the misfortune of falling asleep during committee session and the Chair calls on you, the first words out of your tired, exhausted, sleep-deprived mouth should be a shout of "DIPLOMACY!" Diplomacy is the overarching umbrella that must contain all of your philosophies on Model United Nations.

The Contents of this Chapter Include:
1. *A Brief History of the United Nations*
2. *Structure of the United Nations*

Now that we've explained diplomacy, you must also realize that there are many other important ideals which will need to emanate from your newly diplomatic voice. In order to create your own belief system it is important to surround yourself with as much information about the UN as possible. We recommend that you now read on to **A Brief History of the United Nations** in order to better understand the purpose and goals of this organization. If you are familiar with the history of the UN, you should skip to the next section, Your Role in the Model United Nations.

A BRIEF HISTORY OF THE UNITED NATIONS

Every day the world shrinks in size due to technology and innovation. Oceans and mountains that only fifty years ago were thought to be impassable barriers have proven to be merely inconvenient speed bumps on the highway of global trade. Now more than ever, the United Nations (UN) has been expanding its influence on world affairs and global economy. Your ability to understand the United Nations and its working parts will give you a strong foundation for your future dealings in the Model United Nations.

The United Nations is an organization that was created out of the chaos and power vacuum following the World War I and II. Its forefather, the League of Nations, opened the door for the concept of a world organization dedicated to promoting peace. Proposed by President Woodrow Wilson during the Paris Peace Conference of 1919, the League of Nations was supposed to be the crown jewel of Wilson's plan to reconstruct Europe called the Fourteen Points.

Regretfully, limited legislative power and failure by the United States Congress to approve the Treaty of Paris of 1919 left this entity an empty shell and led to its eventually dissolution. Although the League of Nations failed to create a permanent organization, it did give popularity to the idea that there needed to be a legitimate world body to listen and mediate international crises.

During the late 1930's the world once again was driven to the brink of war. Suffering from one of the worst economic crises ever seen in human history, the Great

Depression, Europeans and Americans were forced to make hard decisions in an effort to return to prosperity. Many choose to sacrifice good sense for stability leading to a rash of dictatorships spread across Central and Eastern Europe. Nations like Germany, Italy, and Japan revived ideas of militarism, imperialism, and conquest and unleashed pestilence and war across globe as never seen previously. For six years, World War II shook the continents of Europe, Africa, and Asia raining bombs, bullets, and genocide on the poor people of the globe.

World War II forced leaders to recognize that they could not repeat this costly pattern of war and reconstruction. Discussions between Prime Minister of Great Britain Winston Churchill and American President Franklin D. Roosevelt as early as August 1941 included plans to create a world organization to avoid future conflicts. This Atlantic Charter, as it was called, created a road map to guide Allied policy to accomplish its post-war goals. These plans were developed and refined by Allied leadership during their future meetings at Moscow, Dumbarton Oaks, and Yalta.

As the war drew to a close, 50 delegates, representing nations from around the world, met in San Francisco in April 1945 to create a new world order. Although many of the original leaders of the Allies had changed, their commitment to this new United Nations had no way faltered. The new American President Harry Truman opened the conference reminding the delegates of the importance of their task at hand, "At no time in history has there been a more necessary meeting than this one... you, members of this conference, are to be architects of the better world. In your hands rests our future.[i]" Tirelessly over the course of the next two months, these fifty delegates completed the charter of the United Nations creating the organization that we have come to know today.

Overall, the goal of the United Nations is to encourage diplomacy. It was created with progressive and utopian ideals in mind and deals with many of the problems that have plagued our society since its inception in 1945. Human rights, economic and humanitarian aid, imperialism, and nuclear disarmament are still issues that are presently debated during committee session.

Regardless of any bias for or against the existence of this institution, it is a wonderful concept to present to high school students. This is the *Model* United Nations [MUN]. Surprisingly, the MUN concept has become an incredible educational force that is transforming some of our most bashful students into leaders, politicians, lobbyists, lawyers, entrepreneurs, executives, and motivational speakers. The skills that students learn through MUN may become the greatest skills they will ever develop.

STRUCTURE OF THE UNITED NATIONS

If you are a complete newbie to this organization, it is important for you to learn the structure of its current incarnation. This information is even more important than the history you've just read about. During conferences you'll always be expected to have some idea of how the United Nations is organized.

The United Nations is considered international territory despite being headquartered in New York City, and maintains three other central offices in Geneva, Nairobi, and Vienna. The cost of operations for the United Nations is internationally funded by "compulsory and voluntary contributions" from the UN's member states. The five members of the Security Council tend to contribute the most funding.

The United Nations main purpose is that of a public forum for debate on international issues. Other aims of the United Nations include facilitating cooperation in international law, international security, economic development, social progress, human rights, and the achievement of world peace. Not everyone agrees with the aims of the United Nations. The administration of former president George W. Bush believed the organization to be weak and ineffective. The new Obama administration has yet to make a clear and defined policy on the effectiveness of the UN.

As a delegate you are typically representing the members of the multiple specialized agencies within the United Nations. There are six principal organs. Here is a quick summary of each to help you get better acquainted.

General Assembly (GA):

According to the United Nations Charter, the General Assembly is the chief policy making body in the United Nations, but that is not true in actual practice. There are 193 nations that make up the General Assembly and are allowed one vote on issues affecting this organ. Nations represented in the General Assembly have the right to recommend actions, debate important world issues, and provide a forum for the injustices of the world.

Security Council:

The Security Council is the most powerful organ in the United Nations. There are five permanent members on the Security Council. These nations include the United Kingdom, France, China, Russia, and the United States. The remainder of the Security Council is composed of ten other regional members that were elected to a two year term from the General Assembly. Permanent members are allowed a special veto power that can stop any action of the United Nations if they so choose.

Economic and Social Council (ECOSOC):

The Economic and Social Council is a little different. Its 54 member council is elected from the General Assembly and serves on a three year rotation. The Economic and Social Council holds influence over international trade, finance, and investment policy.

Secretariat:

The Secretariat is responsible for performing the day to day operations of the United Nations. There are nearly 9,000 staff members spread across the world that help the United Nations perform its various functions. The leader of this organ is the Secretary General. He is the face of the United Nations and is elected to a five year term. The current Secretary General is Ban Ki-moon from South Korea.

International Court of Justice (ICJ):

The International Court of Justice is where the majority of the world's international legal issues are settled. The ICJ is located at The Hague in the Netherlands. The ICJ traditionally settles countless disputes dealing with national sovereignty, war crimes, and even genocide. The United States does not acknowledge the authority of The Hague over its local courts.

United Nations Trusteeship Council:

The United Nations Trusteeship Council was intended to oversee *decolonization* following World War II—decolonization is the process of transitioning dependent nations and former colonies into sovereign statehood. Immediately following the war, eleven nations were placed in the care of the United Nations Trusteeship Council. All eleven of these countries eventually gained their independence or joined with other sovereign nations. Currently, the UN Trusteeship Council has no dependent nation in its care.

Other prominent UN System agencies include:

World Health Organization (WHO)
World Food Programme (WFP)
United Nations Children's Fund (UNICEF)

These organizations are under the umbrella of the GA. Their purpose is primarily aligned with global humanitarian aid and relief.

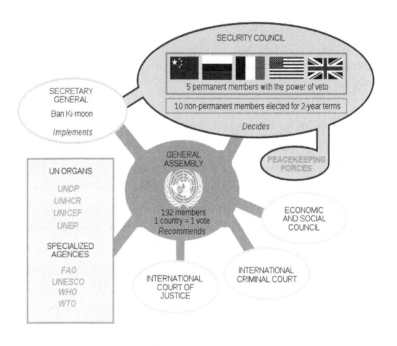

Within the General Assembly (GA), Economic and Social Council (ECOSOC), WHO, WFP, and UNICEF, you may represent any of the current 193 member states (there are minor unimportant exceptions). The member states include every internationally recognized sovereign state in the world but Vatican City.

The other specialized agencies are considerably smaller and have membership that may consist of member states or specific people. You may represent any of the members of those specialized agencies at a conference. There's very little change in the difficulty level within the large committees such as the GA, ECOSOC, WHO, WFP, and UNICEF, but there is a major step in difficulty when you are a delegate in the ICJ or the Security Council. If you're a newbie, start with the "big" committees.

So all in all, with its offices around the world, the UN and its specialized agencies can handle any possible situation across the globe. The World Health Organization (WHO) might debate world policy on AIDS, malaria, cancer, medical technologies, or regional issues. The International Court of Justice (ICJ) may preside over international court cases dealing with the recognition of sovereign states. The General Assembly (GA) might debate the development of international nuclear energy facilities, or they will discuss the most recent civil war in Syria. You will be publicly speaking and debating about these issues if you are a delegate in any one of these committees.

Now that we've shown you the general idea of this organization, we can advance to our next lesson. Other books would now progress to resolution writing, position papers, and Parliamentary Procedures. We have a different philosophy. This may sound crazy, but "rules" are easy. Awards are won with CONFIDENCE and that is the hardest part. It might be the most important skill you can ever learn.

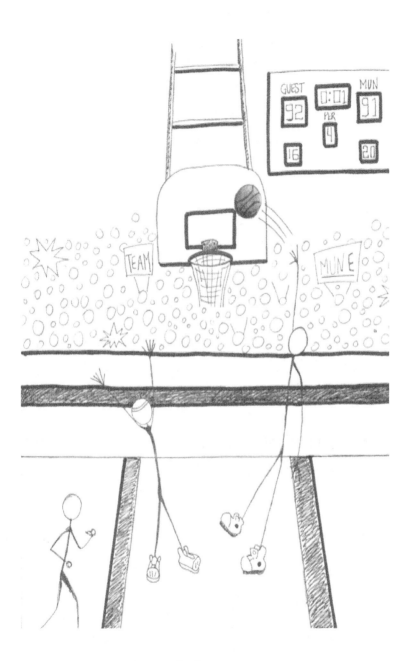

"The Picket Fence"
by Thomas White
12

CHAPTER 2: The Attitude of Winning

It's not a big deal if you lose, but winning is freakin awesome!

When you feel like you are winning, you exude confidence that EVERYONE else notices. This first sentence is the essence to this entire chapter.

Don't misinterpret. There are pitfalls to this 'attitude' if you're not careful with your emotions. You're young, and young people are prone to emotional mistakes ALL the time. It's ok. Everyone has made these mistakes. This chapter will explain how to appear like a winner by describing the most overlooked skills in the entire Model UN arsenal. These techniques will make you more successful at MUN, and can be utilized throughout other aspects of your life.

The Contents of this Chapter Include:
1. *Confidence with Charisma*
2. *The Goal of All Personal Interactions*
3. *The Goal-Oriented Mindset*
4. *The Fine Balance between Selfish and Selfless*
5. *Drills*

You truly will not know whether you understand the concepts until you attempt to put them into practice. In each chapter from here forward, we will include drills for you to practice the techniques described herein. Most of the best delegates have practiced the skills in this book whether they know it or not.

Let us tell you a secret you've probably never

heard: **you can develop and improve every personality trait you've ever wanted to possess, from confidence to brilliance.** It just takes practice.

CONFIDENCE WITH CHARISMA

Before we explain to you what *charismatic confidence* is, we must describe to you what it is NOT. It is **not** arrogance. You are **not** allowed to be the center of the universe. You are **not** the coolest, smoothest, sweetest, most attractive person in the room. If you honestly believe that nonsense, than you will be considered self-righteous, sanctimonious, or any other good SAT word that you might use to berate your opponent in caucus. People who satisfy these adjectives think that they are much more charming than they are, and their confidence immediately changes to a feeling of repulsion! If you improve at "confidence" you'll notice these results. To quote President Theodore Roosevelt, "Speak softly and carry a big stick."

In order to garner results, you must not alienate other delegates by appearing abrasive. This is the essence of diplomacy. To maintain this balance you must be firm in your position, but flexible with your social skills.

Charm (the root of *charisma* and *charismatic*) is the noun that describes the enjoyable feeling from the simple presence of another person. This isn't just about romantic attraction. You need to *like* someone in order to *enjoy* talking to them. Similar to Frodo being twisted by the Ring of Power, people usually do not understand why they're so 'charmed' by you. It just happens.

Since we've explained a little bit about the dark, arrogant side of pride, and we've touched on the magic of charm, we can talk about the balance that makes **real**

14

confidence. It's the good kind of pride. Confidence is magnetic. Every human being is attracted to confidence. Why? Confidence creates more confidence. People who are confident spread calm and comfort to everyone in a room. As one delegate told us, "whenever that kid talks, everyone just stops and listens… I want to be able to do that!"

Let's do an extreme example. Imagine that your favorite band decided they wanted to spend the day with you. That would make you feel kind of special, right? Well, confident people share that aura of accomplishment, success, and desirability. When we are around them, we feel like we are more accomplished, successful and attractive. These traits make us more visible. People notice us when we stand tall, speak strongly, and smile. These are exactly the traits that award winners in Model UN demonstrate.

So how do we train ourselves to "feel" more confident? We'll explain it here first, but at the end of this chapter there are some specific drills you can do to master the attitude of confidence. Here are a few keys to gain a sense of confidence:

1. The attitude of confidence is a belief in which you KNOW that you are **valuable** in a multitude of ways.

2. When the rest of the committee starts to recognize that you believe you are valuable, they will give you the respect that you know you deserve. This becomes a very powerful tool during a committee session because it will feed your confidence exponentially.

15

3. Optimism is a key to confidence. People who are confident do not expect to lose. They already act like a winner in every situation; even when they are unsure about exactly what to do, they still make suggestions and try to solve problems. Winners know that there HAS to be a solution.

4. Do not be overzealous or pushy. Sometimes people who seem confident are actually scared that they will not be noticed or recognized. Confident people do not force their opinions on others because they already know that their ideas are valuable. When one person rejects their ideas, they don't overreact. They know they will find other people who will listen.

5. Confidence will never come across as arrogance if you **look people in the eye** and **treat them with respect**. Practice this at all times. Don't be scared to look people in the eye.

Some of you will need to practice these techniques immediately. The first few drills at the end of the chapter will help you with these five keys to confidence. The drills have been carefully crafted so that you will conquer all of your fears. Speaks, Yoda does: "Do or do not, there is no try."

THE GOAL OF ALL PERSONAL INTERACTIONS

People are creatures, who thrive on social interaction. Every day, you wake up at the same time as your classmates, wear similar clothing, speak the same language, and learn very similar subjects. We are all a part of a large culture that has evolved from a huge number of individuals who collectively agreed to build a system in which (at varying degrees) to conform.

You are bound to this system. You thrive upon the same types of interactions that have been happening among people who share your culture. We are all destined to share our thoughts with one another and communicate. The entire goal of all interaction is simply to communicate. So before we even bother to talk about the details of *what* we communicate to another person, we have to FIRST talk about something MORE POWERFUL. You need to make them *FEEL* good for talking to you in the first place.

YOUR GOAL:
You are to leave every person you talk to feeling better than when the conversation started.

You have to make people feel good. Yes... even the person you're competing against! When they talk to you, make them smile. Tell a small joke to break the ice. Compliment them on how well they spoke the last time they approached the podium. Comment on how you look forward to working together in the future.

You are not just using these lines, you are saying them truthfully. Say nice, optimistic, respectful things that you truly believe. You'll also be communicating with confidence! Not only will they feel appreciated, but you will win their loyalty. Remember that **YOU** are the confident person that they want to be around! Improving these skills will make you an unstoppable force in the committee room.

Don't even worry about the death of the Euro or the war in Afghanistan; we will get to the political issues later. Before we pretend to solve the world's problems, we need to project a positive presence in the room. We need you to feel comfortable communicating with another person, and your fellow delegates need to feel the same way about YOU.

THE GOAL ORIENTED MINDSET

Ok, this piece of the puzzle can be difficult to understand so we are going to start with a little exercise. Let's imagine that a group of us are going to build a house together. Before we start construction, there are a number of details that need to be discussed. Which materials would be needed to accomplish this task? Somebody says "wood," another person yells "concrete," somebody else says "adobe," and a few other materials are also discussed in the room.

What would you suggest? Think about it for a minute and try to start from the simplest possible perspective so that nothing is overlooked. Take a minute, stop reading, and make a few notes about what you would suggest.

We've got something that you may not have thought of: a plan. Did you think to ask how much money is in the budget? Have you thought of the home's purpose? Who will be living there? How many bedrooms or bathrooms? Did you make any of these considerations? The goal-oriented person is not the person who gets to the finish line the fastest. It is the person who thinks about all the little things that need to be finished FIRST. Before anyone should be thinking about the finish line, **you must know** *how* **to get there**. We've coached sports teams who love to think about winning championships, but they never got to a championship game because they didn't do all of the necessary drills to get good enough to be in the playoffs!

Ok, so let's do one more exercise to try and help you get a feel for this idea about goals and success. Let's say you'd like to pursue a career in international diplomacy. Take another minute for yourself, grab a piece of paper and write a step-by-step ladder to that goal.

If the dean of the MUNiversity were planning his career as an international diplomat, these would be his initial steps:

1. He would research exactly what are the responsibilities of an international diplomat.

2. He would take any class that deals with history or international relations that his high school offers.

3. He would create a system to maintain a high GPA. This will allow him to take as many Advanced Placement classes as possible before he graduates.

19

4. He would research the best colleges in the world for international policy, international law, and global economics.

5. Lastly, he would dedicate himself to learning a foreign language as soon as possible.

Did you forget step 1? The only allowable reason for you to skip step 1 is if you are already well acquainted with an international diplomat, or maybe you've written a biography on someone who is an international diplomat. Otherwise, you need to ask the simplest questions first. Preparation is the key to all success. If you fail to perceive the foundation of the problem, you will fail to succeed. "The battle is won before it is fought," –Sun Tzu[ii].

Some of the most successful people in the world knew what they wanted to do when they were young. As soon as that feeling arose, they started practicing their passion every single day. Most of the famous singers, entertainers, and comedians you have heard of were practicing before they were 6-years-old. The goal-oriented person doesn't just have their eye on the prize. They dedicate themselves to paving a road and plotting the route that they need to reach their destination.

The delegate who shows a goal-oriented perspective is the delegate who first realizes that they need a seat in the front and center of committee. Then the delegate starts working on plans to build a network of allies, anticipating the topics of committee and the issues in the background guide. They already have thought about solutions to global issues, as well as a plan for developing a relationship with the chair.

20

THE FINE BALANCE BETWEEN SELFISH AND SELFLESS

In Model UN, and in life, all of us have been pushed to share. As a child, your mom and dad may have yelled at you for being selfish. At birthday parties, you may have wanted the biggest piece of cake, but somebody wouldn't get any if you took that whole corner with all the delicious icing. In school, the teacher cannot spend the entire period only helping you. Now you know all about sharing, or being **selfless**.

Being completely selfless is a very difficult way to win. Yielding time to another delegate means that you are telling the committee that another delegation has something more important to say. If there's only one piece of candy left, wouldn't you feel really special if everyone chose to give it to you? Great! Now you know what it means to be **selfish**!

If you're too selfless, you'll never win the big rewards AND if you're too selfish, no one will ever share any big rewards with you.

Read that sentence one more time and then read on.

Being too selfless: Imagine that you were in a committee session dealing with world hunger. In your everlasting state of compassion you pledge an enormous aid package to a famine stricken nation. Regretfully for the beleaguered people of your country there is really no aid to send. What have you done to the inhabitants of your own country? At what cost did this kind act affect you?

21

Being too selfish: Using the same scenario, let's imagine that you offered zero aid to that suffering nation we previously described. How would you be perceived by the rest of the delegates in the committee? Do you think that this act would be considered diplomatic?

As you can see the extremes of this scenario have resulted in an undesirable outcome for your delegation. Now let's look at how a savvy diplomat would resolve this issue.

The Delicate BALANCE: Selflessly, you have to strike the right chord with people. You have to "sing their tune" or "dance with them" or at least "speak the same language." This requires being a little selfless. Selfishly, you need them to respect your beliefs, security, emotions, and more importantly, you. You need to show that you are a strong individual!

Sports are a perfect analogy. When teams choose a captain, they are choosing someone who is usually good at the sport. They are also choosing the person who BEST REPRESENTS the whole team. In all of my years playing sports, the "captain" usually was NOT the best person on the team. Although they were good athletes, the captains were usually the best example of CHARISMA AND CONFIDENCE.

Confidence is a blend of pride, charm, individuality, assuredness, and poise. You must discover what these adjectives mean for you... Then you'll officially become a Zen master of confidence.

DRILLS

1. Simple drills for overcoming basic fears. These are completely serious. Even if you think you're not a fearful individual, these drills can still be pretty eye-opening.

   a. Look into another person's eyes without making a face for 1 minute.
   b. Say hello to 5 people you don't know. Think of a question that truly interests you, and ask one of these people to respond.
   c. Pick something about yourself that you'd like to change. It must be something you can actually fix. Now come up with a way to fix it.
   d. Take a day where you really listen more than you talk. Then take a whole day where you try to create conversation. Write a few paragraphs about how you felt about those two days.

2. Simple drills for stepping it up a notch. (If you have any problem with the next set of drills, go back and repeat Drill #1 again.)

   a. Have a conversation with yourself in the mirror and take notice of things you REPEATEDLY do, words you REPEATEDLY say, a way you ALWAYS swing your arm, the way you lift your eyebrows, the posture you have when you stand. Go watch a movie with a really strong actor/actress and compare your habits with that person.

b. Have a conversation with someone you wouldn't normally interact with for more than two minutes. Try 5. Make sure that you show them that you respect their opinions and make sure that they know that they should respect yours in a NICE WAY.

c. Think of someone that you don't want to stand up to. Be honest with yourself and write down WHY you don't want to stand up to them... What's holding you back? Fear? What are you scared of? Either accept it and forgive yourself for it, or figure out the reason that you're afraid. We suggest the latter.

d. Have a conversation with someone that you are romantically attracted to but have been too shy to interact with in the past.

"Daniel-son! Ok to lose to opponent; never OK to lose to fear!"
– Mr. Miyagi, The Karate Kid

These drills are about combating your fears. **A winner is fearless.** Now let's learn how to be "Teflon Smooth."

"The Family"
by Thomas White

CHAPTER 3: Teflon Smooth
"Too cool for school, but so gosh darn good at it"

A huge chunk of this chapter holds the keys to successfully influencing all types of people. These keys are powerful if used properly. They are the means to gain favor, win allies, empathize with others, and to earn trust and understanding. These are also valuable techniques that help to develop confidence and leadership skills. By utilizing these techniques, those around you will begin to view you differently. They are long term patterns of behavior that you need to use in order to achieve results. As you attempt some of these strategies we suggest, there might be moments where you question if it's worth the effort to practice these skills.

YOU NEED TO PRACTICE THESE SKILLS
TO SEE RESULTS.

Also, before proceeding, another mention needs to be made. Although we write in an active style, wherein we direct you to speak and act in a certain manner, a TEFLON SMOOTH character seems like they accomplish great things without even trying. These delegates understand how to remain poised and composed in tough situations.

The Contents of this Chapter Include:
1. *BODY LANGUAGE*
2. *VOCAL TECHNIQUES*
3. *RAPPORT*
4. *AWARENESS*
5. *DRILLS*

BODY LANGUAGE

Stand Up Straight - If you slouch, people may develop negative opinions about you. This is something that you can easily avoid by simply maintaining good posture. By standing up straight you appear healthy and confident.

Head – You need to be able project your message and speak to the back of the committee room. Pick your head up. Also, by elevating your head, you are able to better assess what is happening while you are speaking and caucusing. Avoid the "bobble head" because it is distracting the audience.

Facial Expressions –Practice delivering your speech into a video camera to diagnose any subconscious habits. (A mirror can also serve a similar purpose.) Anxiety may cause you to develop some interesting facial quirks. Some people twitch their eyebrows or have a HUGE smile like they're trying to show their teeth to the entire crowd. Some people talk out of the side of their mouth. Try to figure out if you have any of these particular issues. Once you've recognized these habits you can work to minimize their appearance during your speech.

Shoulders –Try to remain relaxed but don't slouch. Avoid stretching your shoulders back so far that it seems that your chest is protruding. Conversely, having your shoulders too far forward may cause you to appear tense or nervous. Find that happy medium between good posture and comfort.

Arms - The arms are tricky because the possibilities are limitless! The arms become like an art form. The first thing you need to do is to get comfortable standing with both arms RELAXED, motionless, and at your sides. We're not saying mimic a robot, but reserve your arm motion for important moments in a speech. Overactive arms are very distracting to the audience. This technique also looks so much better than the delegates that use the "here, hold my pen" hand gesture repetitively during the speech. Remember the other delegates probably already have a pen and they don't need yours. For the best examples of arm motion, watch some standup comedians or some charismatic political speakers.

Don't cross your arms. Arm folding causes you to appear as if you're close-minded and defensive. If you don't know what to do with or arms, do one of these three things:

1. Put them both in your back pockets.
2. Put one in a front pocket and let the other one hang out **RELAXED**. Use it only for important details.
3. Leave both arms **relaxed** at your sides.

Chest, Hips and Legs - The trick to aligning your body correctly is to position yourself according to those around you. When having a conversation, check the floor and look at how people's feet are angled. *Who* are they all facing? If they're facing another person, you should probably face that person, too. If they're facing you, you should face them. If everyone is in a circle, you should face the center of the circle and rotate your head relatively often so each person knows that you're listening. When you speak, you're speaking to ALL of them.

Feet – This is the other tricky appendage when dealing with body language. Men should stand with their feet about shoulder width apart; women usually position their feet a little closer together. Don't fidget, stand straight. Shift your weight one way, then maybe the other way, but don't do that too often. Avoid unnecessary leg movement because you'll appear distracted and immature. You will not appear confident unless you show *poise*.

VOCAL TECHNIQUES

Now, we will talk about your voice because it is the direct connection that demonstrates that you *SHARE* the same emotions as everyone else. Your body language will demonstrate that you have the strength to feel meaningful, strong emotions and that you're capable enough to handle your emotions like a mature person. Your voice is the music that accompanies your diplomatic soul. It must be used carefully. This is definitely a difficult job; however we will share with you a technique called the *S.I.V.* System.

Vocal techniques will first be approached through the idea of speaking to large committee sessions, moderated or unmoderated. The following are the three pieces of the S.I.V. System that you need to **memorize**:

S = *speed, stop, slow down*
I = *inflection, interactive, interesting*
V = *volume, verbosity, victory*

S. *Speed, Slow Down, Stop*

95% of the world needs to SLOW DOWN. You probably need to slow down, too. When you are speaking to someone you don't know, they can't predict your reactions, your accent, and they aren't familiar with any of your pronunciations. You need to make sure they really hear you. Look at them and their faces. Are they paying attention? Are they smiling when you want them to? Maybe they missed what you said because you said it too fast. Maybe they aren't laughing because they don't understand your sense of humor yet.

Also, *pauses actually help.* Recently, there was a scientific study that proved that the "um" that individuals constantly say during conversation was actually helpful to the listener.[iii] We were completely amazed when we learned this fact. We always thought that people would hate the "uh's" and "um's" that slow conversations down. We also thought that the person who said all those uh's and um's was perceived by the listener to be less intelligent than people who don't use those common pauses. So now, instead of saying "um" and "uh," just pause. Stop for a full second after you say something emotional. Give people another second to really hear you and have an emotional reaction.

When you get more comfortable with the pace (*Speed*) of your speech, you'll be able to use small pauses (*Stop*) and a slower pace (*Slow down*) and your words will sound more powerful because of those small pauses before the really emotional punchlines.

I. *Inflection, Interaction, Interesting*

Inflection is probably the most qualitative difference between a good lecture and a bad lecture. Think of your most interesting teacher. Now think of your least interesting teacher. Think about the differences in THE WAY they talk. I'm going to leave it as vague as "the way" for now.

Can you *feel* the difference between someone screaming just to be loud and someone screaming in anger? Notice how we said "*feel*" and **not** "hear." Inflection is the difference between simply "hearing" what someone says as opposed to "*feeling*" what someone says. Good examples of words that require inflection are curse-words. No one ever uses a curse-word without adding emotion and feeling after the word is spoken. Hopefully with this extreme example, you're getting a clue about inflection.

Good speakers are interactive with their audience by the use of inflection. You are not speaking to an inanimate object therefore the inflection you use will impact their response. You can scream at a wall and see where that gets you, but we assure you that if you scream at a person there will be a response. Don't you see that the **listener** is a *HUGE* part of the conversation?

With a large crowd, you have to keep their attention at all costs! Great inflection can help you maintain their interest each time they hear you. Not only do you need a punchline to finish your speech, you have to say it in such a way that it touches everyone!

The inflection in your voice is what makes you seem interactive with the crowd. You are everyone's friend and they all will find you interesting because your voice *feels* so interactive when you speak with each person.

For great examples of inflection, you should close your eyes and listen to several hosts of TV talk shows. TV hosts talk to millions of people every day and they are definitely our modern masters of body language, speech and inflection.

V. *Volume, Verbosity, Victory*

In algebra, you've learned about "variables." Don't get all math-phobic! Stick with us on this one. We're not going to go over the slope-intercept formula. Variables can be as simple as the Treble and Bass knobs on a car radio. They change the sound "equation" and they make your speakers sound different. Anything can be a variable!

In the "equation" for Model UN, there are variables that can change your ability to be heard. These factors can add or multiply together. You might have to shout if everyone is shouting. You might have to whisper when there's twenty people around but you only want one delegate to hear you. You have to use your awareness of those variables to change your volume to an appropriate level. Your volume can make your voice soothing or annoying.

One variable that can affect your volume and speech is a microphone. Have you ever practiced with a microphone? Here is an even better question: have you ever recorded yourself talking? When you speak, do you speak loud enough so that you're SURE that everyone can hear you? If you don't, you should read back about that "confidence" portion from the last chapter. Then, practice talking louder.

33

Verbosity—it means how "wordy" you are—is determined by the time limit, but a good general rule is "short and sweet." The first piece of the S.I.V. System is speed/stop/slow down. You need to say less but say it with more Inflection. Volume control makes the whole package powerful. You must turn down your quantity of word use (verbosity) and turn up the quality of your word choice. This type of ability begins to form as you repeatedly practice all of the concepts here.

The last 'v': **Victory.** Victory is what you will achieve when you use this system. You will know that you have accomplished this goal when you deliver that one last speech: the victory speech. It is the speech that buries the hopes and dreams of your opponents in committee. At that moment, you will know that you've mastered the voice.

RAPPORT

Ideas about rapport stretch from the concept of being friendly all the way to hypnotism. It means you have established a connection with someone. It's like the image that appears on your TV when you've finally connected the cable box. You are "in rapport" when you and another person are *fully* connected and communicating. It means you've agreed on something; it can be a feeling, an opinion, a body posture, or even your breath rate.

In the previous sections on body language and vocal technique, the emphasis was on your actions. For rapport, you need to change your focus and concentrate on the speaker. You need to be an active listener first, a skill that is often not easy to develop. As an active listener you try to observe a person's body language, facial expressions, and their overall demeanor while listening to the information that they communicate. It is a stylistic way to interpret and reflect another person's behavior while helping to establish a connection with them.

It is impossible to establish rapport with another person without creating some type of connection. A 'connection' is when information flows from one location to another similar to the interaction that takes place between a modem and a router in a computer. As long as the modem is plugged into the proper port, a computer can communicate with other machines thousands of miles away. Humans have 'ports' too, but the data passed back and forth are not always patterned and well-defined.

Language is one common example of a port that people use. Conversation allows for the exchange of information and gives each of us an opportunity to establish a connection with another person. Keep in mind that the method you use to transmit your data, e.g. your *dialect*, may be much different than the way we transmit our data. Sometimes people accidentally misuse language and broadcast mixed messages that lead to confusion.

Hopefully you are starting to appreciate how complicated this whole "rapport" concept can be! The reason why it is so hard to establish these connections is because rapport is a TWO-step process. *First,* you need to understand WHY someone is exhibiting a particular mood or behavior pattern. *Second,* you have to show that person that you truly appreciate and understand WHY their behavior pattern or mood is justified.

Sometimes "rapport" is even simpler and more subtle. Sometimes you can just stand with the same exact posture, speak with the same rhythm, and breathe with the same exact pace as another person. That person will *magically* treat you like more of an equal. If you are really good at rapport, you can make friends with your "enemies." All of these are examples of building rapport. Rapport is so important. It can be argued that every Model UN award that has been fairly awarded was judged on the basis of a delegate's ability to establish rapport.

Ok. Now that we've introduced the idea, we need two initial guidelines—precursors to beginning the practice of rapport. These are simple ideas that you need to be aware of so that you can be successful with rapport.

Eye Contact and Emotion:

It is essential to keep eye contact with a person that you're trying to build rapport with. We wear our emotions right on our faces, plain as day, and usually if we are next to someone who we call "friend," that person can tell what our mood is by a simple glance.

In rapport, you are supposed to feel like someone's friend and they are supposed to feel like you are their friend. How would you talk to a friend? Usually, you'd talk to a friend in a totally natural way. You're relaxed and cool. When your friend tells you something funny, you laugh... And when your friend tells you something upsetting, you become understanding. You must reflect a delegate's mood the same way. You must act like a friend with the random delegate who wants to be your ally. Keep comfortable eye contact when they talk to you. If they get happy and excited, get a little excited. Smile. Laugh. If they're angry at how committee is going, say something about your own disapproval of a recent motion that was passed.

The idea of developing a friendship with another delegate might seem like common sense to you, but that's how it *should* sound. Regardless of how easy it is to be nice, there's a huge chunk of people out there who neglect to do these simple things. It seems utterly ridiculous, but we'll bet you can think of at least ten people that just can't "connect." If you can master rapport, you will be able to get along with everyone at the party. And trust us, that lonely person in the corner will never forget you for including them...

Rhythm:

Rushing into rapport never succeeds. It's always better to be patient in these social situations. If you try and force a conversation, you will be expected to lead the interaction and that is NOT rapport, that's usually entertainment. 'Seizing the stage' is an invitation for others to put themselves *in rapport* with you. You're NOT the listener, you're the protagonist. The "practice" of rapport is passive. You are supposed to let the person that you have just met to take the lead in the interaction.

When establishing this rhythm remember that recognizing emotions is important as well. Emotions flow like water. If you can identify these emotions early, it is easy to step into that rhythm or flow of discussion. When you finally feel *in rapport* with someone, avoid redirecting this rhythm. Rhythm is similar to the connection that we talked about earlier in the section.

Now, you can begin trying to be "in rapport." We can't give you much more guidance without you going out and trying to do it on your own. Try becoming friends with someone you don't know (of **your** age, preferably at your school... and NOT ONLINE, that's cheating). Go to the back of committee and chat with a bunch of the "too cool for school delegates". Practice this tactic with a new friend and then read on to our next section about awareness.

A warning about setting your sights too high...
You are whatever you want to be when you have established rapport. Read this again: <u>you are whatever you want to be when you have *established* rapport</u>. Your confidence will give you this power to establish whatever type of relationship you'd like with the person once you have won their trust. If you are hoping to establish rapport with someone of exceptional caliber, you better make sure that you walked into that situation with a plan. Socially intelligent, aware people can chew you up if you don't maintain your composure, demonstrate value, and live up to that person's expectations.

Exceptional people, much like exceptional delegates, all have plans. They act on these plans during the conference and use these strategies to succeed. If you are trying to establish rapport with a leader, you need to demonstrate leadership ability. And it needs to be clear, assertive, and dignified.

AWARENESS

Hopefully, this chapter has opened your mind to details in communication that you never even knew existed. Every lesson should have increased your knowledge on the subject. Body Language should have already made changes in what you've noticed about your own posture and other people's twitches. Vocal Technique should have taught you all about what it takes to be noticed. Rapport should have made you aware of what it takes to use Body Language and Vocal Technique so that you can 'work' an audience. You have been slowly building your awareness of the social programming that runs most people's interactions. Yes, it's pretty much like a programmed computer.

For communication to be practiced at the highest, most *aware* level, the mind needs to be ON and OPEN. We told you that emotions are like water. Well, water can be calm and placid or water can be a tsunami. If you can sense the tsunami, get to high ground before that person unleashes their emotional anguish onto you. If calm and placid is the nature of the situation, calm down and make sure not to splash anybody.

Awareness encompasses a multitude of behavior. It is nearly impossible to expound on the *limits* of awareness. We will simply give some very curious anecdotal evidence of the immense potential within social awareness (and human awareness, in general). Some of these can also be interpreted as *social programs*, much like software downloaded onto a computer.

Strange Patterns in Human Behavior

1. When people are confused, they are more likely to answer "yes" to the following question, regardless of content.[iv]

2. A good segment (NOT ALL) of the general population expresses themselves while subconsciously looking in one of six regions according to the memory. If they're talking about

39

something they saw, they look upward. If they're talking about something they heard, they look left or right. If they're talking about something they felt or a specific memory of a situation, they look downward. Now, you can split these three regions into right and left. If they look up and to their right, they're usually using their memory. If they look up and to their left, they're usually using their creative mind and LYING. Again, this doesn't work for everyone but I'll tell you one thing that does... WATCH THEIR EYES. When people ARE LYING they look back to the same spot over and over and over again. Especially when they haven't thought of how to respond about the lie.[v]

3. A psychologist did an experiment with a person who knew that they were to be interviewed for two hours. For the first hour, the psychologist mimicked the postures of the person. For the second hour, the psychologist initiated the postures. The person being interviewed mimicked the psychologist without any awareness of it.[vi]

4. When a person casually makes contact with another person during a short conversation, the person who was touched has a 60% better chance of having good feelings about the conversation.[vii]

5. When a mother reads to her child in the womb, it has been shown that this baby, after being born, suckles a bottle in rhythm with the mother's reading of the book.[viii]

6. Most people respond pleasantly to a greeting while the rest border on nonchalance. Get over your fear and say "hello" to people.[ix]

7. Have you ever watched someone yawn and it made you yawn, too?

8. When people make eye contact with us, we find them more likeable and attractive.[x]

9. There's a muscle in the eyebrow that only moves when you are genuinely smiling. Fake smiles do not move that muscle. If you want to know if someone is giving you a fake smile, look at his or her eyebrows.[xi]

10. In the Midwest during the 1960's there was an experiment on conducted on students and teachers that coined the term the "Pygmalion Effect." Essentially, a teacher was given 20 new students. The psychologists told the teacher that 10 of the students had a lower IQ than the other 10. The choices were completely random but the teacher didn't know that. By the end of the year, the twenty students' achievement was divided along this completely arbitrary line.[xii]

Not only are these interesting, you can start conversations about them. You probably could start a conversation about anything in this entire chapter! It's amazing how we act as human animals. We adhere to a great deal of social conformity. Try to have a conversation with someone about these ten anecdotes.

41

Debate a few of them. Do you think they are really true? Why don't you try to test them?!

Awareness is discussed in more detail throughout the final chapter of this book. We chose to cover this skill in two sections because you must develop the basic skills first before advancing to more complex strategies. Eventually you will be able to start taking cues from your audience and incorporating that information into your speeches and interactions with other delegates during the conference. You must build up more experience as a speaker and delegate before you try to successfully improvise in the heat of the moment.

DRILLS

Attempt the drills in this section with an open mind. It is important to appear natural while speaking, but don't be afraid to leave your comfort zone while addressing the committee. This entire chapter needs to be treated like a drill. You need to read and reread. We've been practicing some of the techniques listed here for years and everyday we still try to get better. The only advice that we can offer here are some personal exercises to expand your emotional range.

We get better at communication when we learn empathy. We get worse at communication when we feel apathy. The problem with empathy is that you will be challenged to get clear about how YOU feel about things you haven't thought about very often. With that said, give some of these a try in order to gauge your own emotional maturity, sensitivity, and depth. Do most of these in private so you can truly experience YOUR emotions.

1. List some good and bad things that you can honestly say about yourself. Now, imagine overhearing some people say the exact opposite of each and every thing you wrote down. Go through them slowly, one at a time. Now out loud, argue on your own behalf to the people who were speaking about you. Have you been paying attention to your feelings while you did this?

2. Do you have any beliefs? Why do you believe the things you believe? If you don't believe in anything, why don't you believe in anything? Write a little bit about this. Try and really get down to the reasons... ask yourself "Why?" every time you come up with a reason. Can you explain all of these things to a person interrogating you about them? Would you get emotional if they still don't get it?

3. Is there any Model UN issue you really, really stand behind? Is there any political agenda that you truly love? Hate? Write down WHY. Imagine the person who represents the opposite opinion is telling you that you're WRONG. What would you say? Next, go find a positive effect of that person's opinion. We know you don't want to agree with that person's OPPOSITE belief, but you need to exercise the ability to be empathetic to an opposing viewpoint.

One last bit of advice...

Here's a quick failsafe for all of your practices from this chapter: when you get nervous thinking about what the rest of the world thinks about the way you're acting, do this little trick: Imagine that there's a TV camera on you and the whole world is watching you. Then do something crazy and entertaining to freak yourself out of being self-conscious. If you want to leave the audience and run to the bathroom and look at yourself in the mirror, go for it. If you stand your ground after that 'crazy moment,' just make a quick apology to the crowd and laugh at yourself a little. People who can laugh at themselves show others that they have a great sense of humor. They also help others to feel more comfortable and less self-conscious. This is the type of personality trait that everyone likes in an ally.

"All the World is a Stage"
by Thomas White

CHAPTER 4: The Cast of Characters

"Know your enemy!!" - RATM

You will encounter many different types of people while you are engaged in your campaign to pillage the Model UN world. In order to best understand your enemies, we've included a guide describing their strengths and weaknesses.

The Contents of this Chapter Include:
1. *The Newbie*
2. *The Absent Joe*
3. *The International Delegate*
4. *The Veteran*
5. *The Gavel Hunter*
6. *The Activist*
7. *The Diplomat*

The Newbie

"Inexperience is an asset. Embrace it."
(Wendy Kopp, CEO and Founder of Teach for America)

Have you ever watched wildlife TV shows? This type of delegate can be easily compared to a young gazelle learning to walk on the Savannah. They are cute, new, and enthusiastic, but they are constantly surrounded by lions and hyenas waiting to pounce. In the end nature is cruel. Only the strong will survive.

Weak and prone to mistakes, these delegates are easy to identify by their youthful countenance and oversized suit jackets. They are not only new to Model UN, they are new to the game. In many cases they are on their first trip by themselves ever. They stay up late. Eat crazy amounts of weird food at weird times. Lose their wallets. Get homesick. They lack many experiences that older, more seasoned Model UN veterans have. They can be easily manipulated.

The Newbie delegate is always an ally, and the general rule is the slower the gazelle, the quicker the meal. Allow these younger, less experienced delegates to be sponsors on your working paper and reap the rewards. The Newbie delegate will actively advertise ideas for you if you direct them, and you can count on them for votes when you need to pass motions and resolutions. Usually they are no threat to seasoned delegates during question-and-answer periods; you don't need to worry about them stealing the show when introducing your resolution.

It is also important to be aware of the dangers of The Newbie delegate as well. DON'T EVER TRUST THE NEWBIE WITH ANYTHING THAT'S IMPORTANT.

EXAMPLE of a Newbie interaction:
FRANCE: "HEY KENYA... DO YOU MIND BRINGING THE USB TO THE CHAIR? WE NEED TO GET OUR RESOLUTION IN PRONTO!"
KENYA (NEWBIE DELEGATE): "SURE, NO PROBLEM!"

KENYA WALKS SLOWLY TOWARDS THE DIAS BUT IS INTERRUPTED BY THE RUSSIAN FEDERATION.

RUSSIAN FED: "HI COMRADE! I NEED A HUGE FAVOR. CAN I BORROW YOUR FLASH DRIVE SO I CAN SAVE MY RESOLUTION? OUR USB IS BROKEN."
KENYA (NEWBIE DELEGATE): "SURE THING. I WAS HEADING UP THERE, ANYWAY."

KENYA HANDS OVER THE USB. THE RUSSIAN FEDERATION QUICKLY USES THE DEVICE AND RETURNS IT TO KENYA.

RUSSIAN FED: "THANKS AGAIN, COMRADE! MOTHER RUSSIA WILL ALWAYS BE IN YOUR DEBT."
KENYA (NEWBIE DELEGATE): "NO WORRIES. IT WAS THE LEAST I COULD DO!"

KENYA GIVES THE CHAIR THE USB AND WALKS AWAY. 20 MINUTES ELAPSE.

FRANCE: HEY KENYA. YOU HANDED IN THE RESOLUTION…. RIGHT?
KENYA(NEWBIE DELEGATE): YAH, OF COURSE I DID. WHY WOULD YOU ASK THAT?
FRANCE: THE CHAIR SAID IT WASN'T ON THE USB YOU GAVE HER. IT ONLY HAD RUSSIA'S RESOLUTION. WHAT HAPPENED?
KENYA (NEWBIE DELEGATE): UMMM… UMMMM… UMMMM…

Remember these types of delegates are new to the game so they are subject to falling for every dirty trick in the book. Don't put chance into play, and keep this unpredictable delegate's role in the conference limited.

> **Conclusion:** MODERATE RISK – MODERATE REWARD

The "Absent Joe"

"But there are advantages to being elected President. The day after I was elected, I had my high school grades classified Top Secret."

(Ronald Reagan)

I'd hate to be the one to expose the dirty underbelly of the Model United Nations, but at every conference there is a group of delegates that could care less about the actual event. They populate the back rows of the committee room listening to iPods, playing on their smart phones, or flirting with some *"New Friend"* because they look ~Dreamy~. These cats are too cool for school!

For obvious reasons this group is very difficult to negotiate with during a conference. They often represent a substantial number of votes, so it is beneficial to have them as allies. The downside of any dark covenant is that you never really know if they will be there when you need them. It is very difficult to trust them. Please remember that these delegates could have almost any level of preparation before entering the committee. Do not underestimate them. These types of delegates aren't stupid; they're just uninterested. If angered these

50

delegates will suddenly become interested in Model UN, and you will face problems for the remainder of the conference.

The best way to deal with the "Absent Joe" delegates is to speak to them on a personal level. Try to sell *yourself* in these situations, not *the cause* that you're positioning to the committee. At the beginning of the committee session, talk to them about anything that has NOTHING to do with Model UN. During short breaks or while walking to the restroom, ask them if they've seen the Nicki Minaj YouTube Video with the little kids singing. (*SO CUTE!*) Earn their trust. Use notes and stay in contact with them. Your relationship should be bubbly, casual, and social. If you build a meaningful relationship try to bring it to the next level by asking them to yield time to you after future speeches. Under no circumstance should you ever waste any real committee time on this group because even the limited risk is not worth the reward.

Conclusion: LOW RISK – LOW REWARD

The International Delegate
"Go to foreign countries and you will get to know the good things one possesses at home."
(Johann Wolfgang Von Goethe)

The number of International delegates attending Model UN conferences in the United States has grown substantially over the last ten years. Recently, at the North

American Invitational Model United Nations, hosted by Georgetown University, there were schools present from Brazil, China, the Dominican Republic, Turkey, Pakistan, Lebanon, Taiwan, and Egypt just to name a few. A casual analysis of attendance at HMUN (Harvard Model United Nations) and ILMUNC (Ivy League Model United Nations Conference) will support this trend. Due to this fact, we have decided to take an in depth look at this group of delegates because if their attendance at American conferences continues to grow you will be forced to interact with these delegates more often in the future.

In the past, the International delegate has not been a legitimate threat at the awards ceremony because of poor proficiency in English and limited fluency. It was quite possible ten years ago to encounter International delegates that did not speak English well. These were near unsurpassable barriers for early International delegates as a whole. The new and improved 2010 International delegate can communicate much more effectively than previous years. (We attribute these advances to globalization, Internet, and film.) Now couple this new found skill in language with a cosmopolitan world view, and suddenly the International delegate starts to grow teeth.

The International delegate still starts at a disadvantage at major Model UN Conferences. No other delegate will face more adversity than the International delegate. Thousands of miles away from home, these delegates are far away from their homes and familiarity. Much like the German armies in World War II, these delegates experience more difficulties the further they are stretched away from their supply lines. Homesickness, fatigue, and language are common issues for International delegates.

To combat these disadvantages, delegates are forced to arrive three days early simply to adjust to the change in time. These are just some examples of the off-the-field issues that the International delegate has to deal with during the conference. Committee selection is important to this group of delegates. If these delegates are trapped in a large General Assembly Committee, the limited speaking time can damage their overall effectiveness. Many International delegates need several speeches to feel comfortable and find their rhythm.

Working with International delegates has both advantages and disadvantages. There will be break downs in communication when you deal with these delegates. Sometimes these language barriers, real and conjured, can affect your working relationship. Defend your work at all times. Don't allow these delegates to take credit for your work because they don't understand the terms of the agreement. One positive of an alliance with this group includes projecting a benevolent image across the committee. Its good practice of public relations to keep them included in your resolution. You will also benefit from their caucusing if you can utilize their skills properly.

Conclusion: MODERATE RISK – MODERATE REWARD

The Veteran

"We all learn by experience but some of us have to go to summer school."

(Peter De Vries)

"So close, yet so far." That's a good way to sum up the Veteran. These delegates are dangerous because they have attended numerous conferences. They are aware of the rules of engagement. However, despite these varied experiences the Veteran is still searching for the proper formula to win a conference. In situations when they need to be aggressive, they are passive. In other situations that require diplomacy, they preach war. Something is always missing for the star crossed Veteran that prevents this delegate from experiencing complete success. Because of this fact, the Veteran is often left wanting at the awards ceremony. Only winning the occasional verbal commendation or honorable mention, the Veteran has never been able to put it all together to win the coveted gavel.

It is hard to trick this type of delegate because they have already been burned a few times in the past. Don't even try. If you can convince a few of these delegates to work as your ally, you will benefit greatly. They usually have good ideas to contribute to potential working papers and can contribute by speaking "intelligently" on behalf of your cause.

Protect yourself from potential treason by keeping this delegate busy. They can brainstorm ideas for working papers or serve as your propaganda minister. We're not telling you to protect yourself because the Veteran is untrustworthy. That is a false assumption. There are only a few people you can actually trust in any committee room. Choose your friends carefully at all times.

If this group decides to work against you during the conference, realize that they're an enemy that is not to be taken lightly. Due to the fact that they've attended so many of the conferences, they know a variety of ways to tie up your working papers and draft resolutions. Many of the Veteran delegates are decent speakers. Try to avoid having them speak openly against you during committee sessions. Remember that there aren't very many of these delegates filling the committee room. There are only a few schools that will travel to multiple national conferences. Any Veterans that you collect as allies will serve as valuable assets. The Veteran will hasten your ascent to success.

Conclusion: LOW RISK – HIGH REWARD

The Gavel Hunter

"And Cain talked with Abel his brother: and it came to pass, when they were in the field that Cain rose up against Abel his brother, and slew him..."
(Genesis 4:8)

The Gavel Hunter is the most dangerous creature that walks the halls of any Model UN Conference and should be feared at all times. These delegates are out to further their own interests at any cost. The best Gavel Hunters are able to blend in well with the rest of the committee making them even more difficult to identify.

The Gavel Hunter is treacherous, so BEWARE! They will destroy your chances of victory in a heartbeat if you allow them the opportunity. Your mission, if you choose to accept it, is to avoid these delegates at all costs and sniff out their cunning ruses meant to deceive you.

Characteristics of a Gavel Hunter:

- They are dressed in Western Business Attire.
- They are intelligent *but can be ill-prepared. (Note: Your cue to strike!)*
- They are persuasive speakers.
- They have MUN-IQ.
- They are Machiavellian. They will break alliances if it suits their interests. They are always looking for a better deal.
- They are social. They bounce from group to group looking for allies to later deceive.
- They are competitive to a fault. Winning is a sickness to them. They will lie, cheat, and steal to accomplish their goal.
- They are devious.
- They are a dangerous enemy that deserves respect.

There are a variety of tactics that a Gavel Hunter will use during the course of a Model UN conference. These tactics range from simple to devious. The best way to prepare yourself to face these nefarious foes is to learn to think like the Gavel Hunter. Here are a few examples to help you on your journey.

The Gavel Hunter will pre-write working papers. Don't let this "fact of life" catch you by surprise. The best way to avoid this pitfall is to simply BE PREPARED for the conference. We know this theme is recurring, but it is so important in becoming a successful Model UN delegate. Try to brainstorm ideas for potential working papers and speeches prior to the conference. (*It's a good practice to even have a few generic pre-written speeches sitting around. You never know when you might catch a yield from another delegation. You'll need some quick inspiration.*) This ready-to-use list of "inspiration" is a valuable tool in the early stages of any MUN conference. Use it to defeat the cheating Gavel Hunter. Out scheme the schemer through preparation. When you catch them screwing up, point it out and never let them live it down.

It is not uncommon for the Gavel Hunter to spread rumors to create turmoil and chaos. There is no denying the extreme power of rumors if allowed to spread unchecked. Rumors have claimed the lives of entrepreneurs and politicians alike. Ask any CEO about the power of these soft whispers. They are the catalyst for hostile takeovers and the harbinger of "change" in the business world. Politicians have been sabotaged by simple murmurs of corruption or impropriety. This powerful weapon will spread across a committee like a pandemic if you allow it.

There are two ways to defend yourself against rumors in committee. Begin by surrounding yourself with a group of competent, loyal delegates. Your ability to be social and build consensus will help you greatly in accomplishing this task. Their trust in you is essential. Don't give them any reason to doubt you at critical moments. Do not burn any bridges with anyone (except the *gavel hunter*) during the early portions of the conference. When the time comes, **stomp** out rumors. The longer they are left to sit, the more dangerous they become. **Prove authenticity** if necessary but above all else, keep good relations with the chair.

Again, avoid this delegate at all costs. The Gavel Hunter is a master of the Dark Arts and will wield his or her evil powers against you mercilessly. Any deal you make with them will be broken. They will steal the spotlight whenever possible. Don't let the Gavel Hunter take credit for all of your hard work, and don't fall prey to this predator of the MUN jungle.

```
Conclusion: HIGH RISK - NO REWARD
```

The Activist

"The day will never come that we forsake this planet and its people."
(Optimus Prime, Transformers III)

World Peace is possible... you just need to believe it! This is the motto of the dogged Activist. Don't misinterpret this philosophy for life as a sign of weakness. Celebrities like Angelina Jolie, Brad Pitt, Tim Robbins, Sean Penn, and Oprah Winfrey have already demonstrated the power of this group in real life. The Activist is a strong adversary that you will encounter during your campaign for Model UN supremacy. These delegates are intelligent and well-spoken, and have a persistent determination that other types of delegates lack. Once the Activist locks on to its target, much like Superman, they swoop in to fight injustice, poverty, and tyranny all across the globe.

58

The trouble with challenging the Activist delegate is that they always enjoy the moral high ground in arguments. The positions that Activist delegates represent embody the core principles of the United Nations. It's beautiful to watch a skilled "Activist" delegate at work. They are able to enchant committee rooms with a vision of an ideal world where consensus and harmony reign supreme. The Activist delegate is often the champion of the developing world. Their arguments are always moral in nature.

It is hard to fault the Activist in their narrow purpose. The issues these delegates represent are the reasons the United Nations exists in the first place. For example, the power and effectiveness of the Activist in committee derives directly from the seriousness of the topic that is being discussed. The more serious the issue, the stronger the delegate is in committee. Often these delegates are the lone voice in the committee room clamoring for recognition of a down-trodden people thirsting for freedom. It's hard to argue against the justness of their cause. The Activist truly fights social ill.

There are weaknesses to the Activist delegate as well. The Activist is prone to losing sight of the main objective of the committee. Activists tend to charge toward their individual objectives like a racehorse with blinders, so it is important to keep their expectations for funding grounded. Often they neglect to consider economic issues in their resolutions. Delegates that are able to craft resolutions using more foresighted provisions are able to out-perform the Activist in many conferences around the country.

Don't make the mistake of following these delegates in their quixotic pursuits. It will best serve you to use these delegates as a means to an end. One simple strategy is to put yourself in opposition to the Activist. Try to argue against the Activist-led working paper on purely economic and financial reasons. Remember that Activists are passionate about their cause. Midway through the conference, break from your original position and try and strike a compromise with the Activist. Most chairs want to see the exercise of diplomacy and compromise when deciding awards. Position yourself as a mediator, and you will reap the rewards at closing ceremonies. If you want to try and include the activist in your consensus early, include humanitarian and eco-friendly provisions in your resolutions. Don't sell the house in order to get their support, though.

```
Conclusion: MODERATE RISK - MODERATE
             REWARD
```

The Diplomat
"Diplomacy is the art of letting someone have your way."
(Daniele Vare)

Attention ladies and gentlemen! We are proud to present tonight's main event. Coming to the ring is the undefeated champion of the world. This delegate is by far the strongest and most effective of all Model UN delegates. He/she is a man/woman that needs no introduction. It is my pleasure to give to you the Diplomat.

The Diplomat is a POWER delegate. There really aren't any flaws to their game, so it is difficult to game plan against them. The Diplomat delegate has the skills and determination to win any conference across the nation. If we were talking about sports we'd be referring to a five-tool athlete: Speech, Intelligence, Writing, Charisma, and SWAG.

These delegates are comfortable in almost any situation because of the variety of weapons they have in their arsenal. They are able to quickly draw topics into their sphere of influence because of their ability to caucus and speak. Despite these huge strategic advantages, the Diplomat will never look to completely dominate a conference through sheer power. This delegate never forgets the cardinal rule, "Might does not make right in Model UN." Instead this delegate manipulates the committee and guides it the direction that he chooses. Much like a stream, the Diplomat doesn't look to move the rock but simply flows around it in perfect motion.

The Diplomat excels in Model UN because he / she is able to have his way without letting people know it. These delegates have a presence when they speak that other delegates just lack. The Diplomat delegates lead without leading. They delegate responsibility and authority to other delegates increasing their power and importance in committee. They **broadcast** a message of compromise during a conference while other delegates just get up and speak. In many instances they act as facilitators and mediators during conferences (this is a great tactic because it places you in the center of an issue demanding extra attention). When critical moments appear, they are able to represent a position of diplomacy that lingers in the judges' minds. Their years of experience allow them to identify these situations early, leaving them time to swoop in and take advantage.

Now don't mistake the Diplomat for a complete push over. We know we repeated phrases about compromise, but the diplomat doesn't just concede his entire country's position. This delegate is aware of his country's policy and knows its limitations. These delegates reserve important moments for their leadership and direction. In many ways they are similar to Niccolo Machiavelli's idea of a leader:

"A prince (leader) should emulate a lion's strength, power, ferocity, and intimidation, but add to that a fox's cunningness, slyness, understanding, and perceptiveness. Since a lion cannot defend himself against traps, and a fox cannot defend himself against wolves, one must be a fox in order to discover the traps, and a lion in order to scare off the wolves. Relying on just one or the other is not enough."[xiii]

It is hard to maintain this balance, but it is essential for success. The Diplomat works in subtlety and inference much like artists work with oils, tempera, or pastels. These delegates will never directly crush their opponent, but realize that many of their loyal legions will jump at the chance to prove their loyalty.

The Diplomat can be beaten, but it is hard to do. You need to knock the Diplomat out of his element and make this delegate appear "un-Diplomatic." It is also important not to be dragged down with the undiplomatic Diplomat if you happen to be successful. You can always try to table their resolutions, but that is equivalent to dropping a nuclear bomb in a committee. Feelings will be hurt afterwards. There is no escaping it.

YOUR GOAL: Become the Diplomat
"Om Mani Padme, Munnnnnnn..."

"Deep Thoughts"
by Thomas White

CHAPTER 5: Rhetoric and Dialectic

Definition: The art of investigating or discussing the truth of opinions

In Model UN, you will be practicing the art of discourse *ALL OF THE TIME*. Discourse (the act of discussing ideas) is a very easy concept. The problem is the difficulty of *mastering* discourse. It can be said that the best delegates in committee are always using persuasive speech (**rhetoric**) and discussing the truth of everyone's opinions (**dialectic**). Some delegates are so masterful at discourse that they force you to question your own opinions. After you hear their arguments, you start wondering about whether you're making the right decisions. This is the end result of mastering the skill of "rhetoric and dialectic."

We don't want you to waste time trying to convince the world that your opinions are true. Instead, you should push other people to *continually second-guess their own opinions*. Through this process, you will be able to investigate all other opinions that have been shared in committee. Then you will slowly introduce opinions of your own that your audience will progressively gravitate towards. This is the sneaky way to be noticed, and it's much more effective.

Before we begin, we want you to first understand the weight of the ideas in this chapter. You are going to attempt to **CHANGE PEOPLE'S MINDS** on controversial issues. Changing someone's opinion on an issue changes *everything* in a relationship. All of your conversations with them will be different from that point forward. <u>The bigger the idea, the bigger the change.</u>

Second, changing someone's mind about a big idea is NOT an easy thing to do. When people believe in an idea, it is not easy to be sure how strongly they believe in that idea. Sometimes if your opinion is different from others presented during a discussion, it may not be very popular in a group of "new" acquaintances. We strongly suggest that you read the section of "rapport" before you try most of the strategies in this chapter. When you attempt to change people's minds, you **MUST** be "in rapport" on SOME level. No one ever changes his or her mind for an opponent. It is also very unlikely that a person will ever change their mind for a stranger. You must seem like a potential friend and/or a powerful ally. Otherwise, it is doubtful that you will be a persuasive presence in committee.

A quick note, a potential warning, and a reminder:

This book has been intentionally organized so that you can become the best possible negotiator, ally, and delegate. Try to attack the chapters in this book in their original sequence. If you try some of the concepts in this chapter without being aware of the ideas presented earlier, you will likely fail. If you push too hard with the wrong person, you will lose negotiations, debates, allies, and it is even possible to lose a friend.

Remember, the goal of all interaction is to leave your audience feeling better for having had a conversation with you. If you change someone's mind on an issue happily and willingly, then you have done your job, and you are achieving the goal of this chapter.

The Contents of this Chapter Include:
1. *THEORY*
2. *EXAMPLES AND DRILLS*
3. *RHETORIC & DIALECTIC IN COMMITTEE*

THEORY

Let's draw a diagram:

The UMBRELLA
Idea

Unified   *Opposing*

Your Argument   Their Argument

There are three points.
1. Your Argument – The opinion you are choosing to support.
2. Their Argument – The idea that is preventing *more* support.
3. The overarching "**<u>umbrella</u>**" idea that gives birth to these two different perspectives.

Simple Example:
Your argument: AIDS is the most important health issue in the world.
Our argument: No, nutrition is the most important issue.
Umbrella: AIDS is a problem because it costs money and millions of lives. There are many issues that are problematic to the world population's health, of which AIDS and malnutrition are important examples.

We can argue over and over again, but if we can agree about the umbrella argument, we can then propose a solution. Our solution would reflect BOTH of our beliefs. We'll BOTH feel better for having argued about AIDS and malnutrition because we united to reach "common ground" as a group, agreeing that BOTH of our arguments are legitimate. In Model UN, the first person to *intelligently and cohesively* propose this agreement usually becomes the "Go To" delegate and gains a big advantage over the rest of the committee. That person is building consensus. *Consensus is **power** in Model UN.*

Another quick example to illustrate a few different ideas:
Your argument: MTV is awesome.
Our argument: MTV is horrible.
Umbrella: What is "MTV?" A TV channel? An advertising agency? A brand based on the combination of music and video? (*This is hilarious because they don't even play music videos anymore.*) Essentially, MTV is now owned by Viacom which is a corporation that aims to make money. If they own a large enough demographic, regardless of the details, they will make money. Whether we like it or not, MTV is very profitable and so well branded that our opinions about this topic don't even matter. You like it? Cool. We

hate it, but we appreciate their success in winning your admiration.

This last example is pretty cheesy, but we're using it to demonstrate the kind of argument that has ZERO substance. The simplicity of "liking something" is as uninteresting as a light's on/off switch. We can make **no** practical use of this conversation unless we are doing market research for MTV or some other sort of applicable research on TV audiences and their watching habits. Please... Don't waste people's time with this sort of discussion and don't EVER assume that they will find you 'smart' or 'impressive' if this is the best conversation you can offer.

Where Model UN is concerned, this type of opinionated discussion should only be used in establishing rapport. And if we were trying to establish rapport with you, we would've gone straight to the *umbrella* idea. We would completely bypass the fact that we do not like MTV. With the goal of rapport in mind, we would have quickly mentioned something stupid... like "people love Jersey Shore." We maybe would've said, "VH1 and a bunch of other channels are owned by a huge company that runs MTV; my friend did an internship there." We would've asked, "do they ever show music videos anymore... Cause I really don't know?"

Take a few seconds and imagine a likable person saying those three things to you. Reread them until you can actually imagine yourself having that conversation. How would you respond? Would you be able to continue the conversation? Would you keep talking to them about how much you love MTV? Or would you have moved onto another topic?

Now that you've *imagined* this little dialogue, we're

now going to tell you the strategies we use when responding to opinions. Despite the fact that we think MTV sucks and that this entire conversation is utterly useless, we still used the following strategies of rhetoric and dialectic:

1. We never disagreed with you.
2. We talked about a topic that you're already talking about.
3. We steered your thoughts into the "Umbrella Idea."
4. We avoided a "like/dislike" argument so we can quickly move onto more enlightening topics.
5. Notice how our chosen question allows us to start promoting our own opinion. It was presented to you in a very different way:

"Why do they call it 'MTV/Music Television' if there's never any music on it anymore? We miss the music!"

This sort of strategy with rhetoric and dialectic will become natural to you as you practice. If you can understand this example and our responding strategy, try it with a friend. You'll learn a lot if you practice each strategy and then review our notes.

As a quick connection to previous chapters, this last example is a strategy that is often used to "open" a person into rapport. When "opening" someone, the subject of the chat can seem difficult. If a delegate opens with a topic for conversation, the subject is chosen for you. You must simply be *clever* about **when** you *insert your commentary*. When overhearing an exchange, you have the choice to watch or to become a valuable contributor to the discussion.

The MTV argument was not only a straightforward example of the three points of the diagram; it was also an example of a clever way to enter a conversation. The strategic use of rhetoric and dialectic is the reason it works so flawlessly.

Origin of Rhetoric and Dialectic: Ancient Greeks and Hegel

In ancient Greece, math was not known by a large segment of the population, education was a new idea, and not many people knew how to use their abilities to argue. The art of discourse and argument was just starting to be investigated by the small group of "Academics" — the word "academic" comes from the name of Plato's school "The Academy". The Greeks gave birth to philosophy, derived from the words "philos" and "Sophia," that translate into English as "the love of wisdom."

Remember that during this era barter and trade was the foundation of the economy. Most traders and merchants were horrible at negotiation, and as a result rhetoric was formed. A family would save money to put their son into one of the small, prestigious schools of the time so the child could learn how to argue as a means of advancing the entire family's economic status. The family would use their child's new skills to improve their quality of life. These kids would argue their families out of debt. In some cases these successful children would argue themselves into politics.

During this time period many different opinions were formed on effective forms of negotiation and debate. Philosophers like Socrates, Plato, and Aristotle discussed dialectic and rhetoric at length. The Socratic Method is one

71

example of pure dialectic and you should start identifying the teachers in your school who teach "Socratically." These teachers are constantly using questions to provoke your inquiry into the heart of the concept being taught. Some teachers are so good at this that they can coax you into teaching yourself.

Several philosophers have proposed dialectics very similar to the threefold diagram we have presented to you. The triangular relationship proposed by Georg Friedrich Hegel referred to our diagram as the "Abstract-Negative-Concrete" or the "Immediate-Mediated-Concrete" model. The "Abstract" is your argument, the "Negative" is their argument, and the "Concrete" is the overarching Umbrella Idea.

Another philosopher, Chalybaus, continued to use Hegel's model, but he called it the "Thesis-Antithesis-Synthesis" threefold relationship. We find that label to be the easiest to understand in light of our description of Rhetoric and Dialectic. This triangular relationship is dependent on finding symmetry between arguments. If you start to look at arguments in this manner, you will have a great advantage in debate and negotiation. When you read through the following examples, keep this symmetry in mind.

EXAMPLES& DRILLS

The next section is presented in as examples followed by drills. You can't practice these alone. You need someone to play "counterpoint" to your arguments. These example arguments will start with abstract topics and become more concrete as you progress. We need to foster an **open mind** in order to help you build your argumentative skill set.

Example A:

Karl Marx made the argument that the "thesis-antithesis-synthesis" argument was made with the impression that a group of gods gifted it to the human race. Another way to put it, Hegel's threefold model was a representation of the archetypal Platonic world and that we automatically use this higher order symmetry, as if it was Divine intervention. Marx was a "materialist." He suggested, rather, that we humans observe the universe first. Only then do we begin to use our brains and translate our observations through what we decide is a *thesis*. After this, we make an empirical decision to acknowledge an *antithesis* to our *thesis*. Then, through further discussion and argument, the learner arrives at a *synthesis* of their previous paradigm and decides it was a result of his or her own *thesis-antithesis* recognition.

Drill: This is another difficult concept. Your second drill is to make sure you understand this Marxist concept (LOOK IT UP!). Secondly (and MORE importantly), make sure your friend understands it, too.

Example B:

This is going to be very specific to politics. Socialism and Capitalism are two opposing economic views on what is the best way to organize a nation's economy. Capitalism is the idea that the "free market" regulates itself. It is a competitive barter and trade system where consumers decide what they want and "businesses" sink or swim depending on whether they offer a legitimate service or product. At its best, it's Denmark. At its worst, it is the plutocracy of United States in the first twenty years of the 1900's.

In contrast to Capitalism, Socialism dictates that the government regulates and determines the products and services that are necessary. At its worst, it's Communist North Korea. At its best, present day Scandinavia. Both types of economies are open for corruption, and both have the potential to develop strong communities and even nations.

Drill: These two economic structures should have been discussed in your history class a few times by now. It's time to really push these ideas. With your friend, jot down at least five pros and cons of each economic system. For every pro, come up with an example (research the internet to find good examples if you can't come up with the examples on your own). For every con, come up with an example or two. Remember, do this part together.

After you've done this brainstorming and research, flip a coin. If you get heads, you get Capitalism and vice versa. Now, take two minutes to think about how you'd argue for your system. Your friend will argue against you. Argue for at least 10 minutes. Make sure you use your brainstormed arguments and examples. As you begin to feel more comfortable, add some of your own examples and opinions into the debate. Be creative. If you can have a smart person witness this conversation, ask them to judge who did a better job. This conversation should be much easier than Examples A and B.

Example C:
OK, this is your chance to have the stupid conversation. You should already know enough about

your friend that you know of something he or she doesn't like as opposed to something that the both of you like. It could be a color, a TV show, a singer, whether you floss before or after you brush... whatever.

Drill: Start the conversation already. Have it for at least 5 minutes. Have FUN! Make fun of each other's opinions, laugh about it. If one of you gets mad or takes something personally, that person needs to go back and read about confidence and self-esteem in Chapter 2. Remember, this conversation is totally inconsequential and useless! (SAT word: *innocuous*. This topic is *innocuous*.) As you had this conversation, did you feel like you were getting smarter? More open-minded? Did you think at some point, that your opinion would make the world a better place?

If you can laugh about your own opinions, you are WELL on your way to being able to talk to any random person in the whole wide world... and have them feeling better for having talked to you. This goal of interaction still needs to be your vision. These drills are meant to open your mind to a different breed of logic and persuasion. Mostly, these are learning exercises. Through the examples you are meant to have legitimate discourse with your buddy. This way you can get into the habit of challenging yourself with these conversations.

Rhetoric and Dialectic in Committee

In committee, you should use the concepts of Rhetoric and Dialectic during any arguments that may surface throughout the committee session. In between committee sessions, you should be reviewing the day's negotiations. Analyze the arguments of the leading delegations in your committee. Study them through the lens presented to you in the Examples section. The thesis-antithesis-synthesis *symmetry* is very useful for professional dialogue, negotiation, and debate. We've approached it from a theoretical sense but now we are going to make this concept much more practical.

We're now going to apply our concept to an individual who works in the business world. Even in the United Nations, delegates are forced to "do business" with one another over a variety of issues. Because of this fact we've decided to provide you with access to a few secret weapons to help you create good situations for "business" in the Model UN world.

The Analogy to a *Sales* Job

In a way, you are always marketing yourself. We can definitely debate whether this is a positive or negative, but this is neither the time nor the place for such a discussion. Here's an example that you should all be able to recognize, Facebook. On Facebook, each person has their own page, their own pictures, their own logo, their own friends. In many ways they are marketing their social value.

If you worked in marketing or sales your responsibilities as a representative would include presenting the merits of your company's services and products. Your client has needs that you must satisfy. You maintain a relationship with your contacts at their business and you make sure all of the details run smoothly. They should be happy and satisfied, and you should be happy to handle their concerns.

When you are a sales representative, you need to

manage two types of relationships. These two realms can be described as social and professional. The professional aspect requires negotiation, compromise, and barter based on the mutual needs of the client. This requires strong detail-oriented discussion much like what has been previously stated in the chapter. The other aspect of this relationship is social and friendly.

The *Social* Aspect of a "Business" Relationship

The dynamics of this social relationship can become quite complex. We can almost guarantee that your idea of a social relationship has only had the goal of pleasure. Usually it appears nonchalant when you chat with your friends, but when developing a *sales* relationship there are many other goals in mind.

Let's do a thought experiment. Imagine that you are a representative for a HUGE company that supplies the labels for cans and bottles. Let's say that you are the *sales* rep who manages the accounts with several companies like Coca-Cola, Tropicana, and Campbell's. This is a small list of the people (*representatives*) you'd have to develop a relationship with from each company:

1. The person who negotiates prices with businesses who sell labels.
2. The person who represents the design team that created the image on the label, the material it's made of, the color of the plastic bottle, the number of bottles needing to be labeled, etc.
3. Their boss or bosses.
4. Your own company's supply manager.
5. Your own company's engineers who tell you whether your company can satisfy the customer's desires. Most customers will have an imagination

that anything is possible; their optimism is usually wrong and you have to tell them that, nicely.

6. You have to talk to the bottle manufacturer who makes all the bottles for those companies. Did you think Tropicana, Coca-Cola, and Campbell's make their own bottles and cans? They don't. The companies that make the bottles have their own sales people, too... and yes, you'll be expected to manage a relationship with them as well.

OK, that's enough... We can go even further, but there's no need. These people have hard jobs and they are socially and professionally connected to tons of other business people. When you are managing an account, you are expected to make sure that your company keeps selling lots of labels. If a company stops buying your labels, your bosses will want you to know why.

Sometimes, the company who is buying labels from you will have a plan that they are going to stop selling a particular product in the near future. They are already planning the bottles and labels that they will sell twelve months from now. If Coca-Cola decides that they're going to stop selling their version of orange soda (*Fanta*) and your company makes the *Fanta* labels, your boss is going to need to know why there weren't five million labels ordered for next year! One of the engineers from Coca-Cola might know that the executives have this plan. It is YOUR job to know all of this information...

If you have a bad relationship with that engineer, he's never going to tell you about the whole *Fanta* situation. You are going to be responsible when your company loses $500,000 for all of the canceled labels that you didn't know about. Sales people work their magic by having "social" relationships with the people who are "in the know." Companies are very aware of these types of situations. They pay their salespeople very well for maintaining these social relationships.

If you are the sales rep for this label company, they will encourage you to take the representatives from other companies out for lunch. You will be expected to have informal chats about their families and friends. Salespeople will ask their "business associates" about their kids and their bosses... they do it nicely; they become their friend. They have *innocuous* conversations because it is easy and fun! People don't want to talk about work all the time.

Applying the Sales Framework to Model UN – The Balance between Social and Professional Relationships

OK, thought experiment over. Now that you know all about "sales", we're going to give you an opportunity to apply this to Model UN. You will form business relationships all day, every day. You will work on problems and speak professionally. In between, you will also make little jokes with one another, talk about opinions, laugh about how bad all of the delegates dress... you talk "socially!" Try to start conversations with your "new" business partners. Ask them about their school. Ask how many people are in their class. Have a friendly relationship! Establish *rapport*. You are marketing yourself.

We've now applied the concepts of Rhetoric and Dialectic to the two major types of conversation. We've shown you how to establish yourself. You have to take advantage of your first impression in both instances. If someone starts a "professional" conversation with you, get down to business and get serious and be serious. If committee hasn't even started yet, be "social" with people. They will remember you. And they will be willing to talk business with you if you have already showed them that you can handle both types of relationships, "professional" and "social". They will also tell you other people's secrets if they know how valuable you are in helping them accomplish their business goals.

Drill: There is only one drill for this part of the chapter. At your next Model UN conference, team up with a "new" partner. Choose someone you've never worked with before. Work hard and do your part to be successful in committee. Make sure you maintain a friendly relationship with your new partner. Pay very special attention to the professional-social balance that you have to maintain *in order to accomplish your business!* Help her and other delegations in accomplishing the goals of committee.

When you begin using our techniques, random strangers might end up being more than just an ally; they might also tell you inside information, too. They might tell you their own personal strategy. They might introduce you to other new allies. They might even turn into long-term friends who will work with you at future conferences.

"Light Work"
by Thomas White

CHAPTER 6: The Blueprint
"Like Ocean's 13... but not an overdone sequel"

There are many different strategies that a person or team can use when competing in a Model United Nations conference. Strategies for individuals can be used in any format of committee. When you are a member of a double delegation, you can use the individual strategies as a delegation or you and your partner can administer two strategies separately.

The *group strategies* are specifically for situations in which two separate delegations are from the same school. You and your "opponent" can collaborate to co-create an advantage in large committees. It's always interesting when two or more delegations **purposely** try to manipulate the course of debate. By the end of this chapter, you should be better at recognizing and implementing these important strategies during a conference.

The Contents of this Chapter Include:
1. *Strategies for Individuals*
   a. *The Hook*
   b. *The Peacock*
   c. *Mediation*
   d. *UNICEF*
   e. *Advanced Placement*
   f. *The Postmaster*
   g. *The Cheerleader*
   h. *Acronyms*

2. *Strategies for Teams*
   a. Ping Pong
   b. Overwhelm
   c. Avoid Crisis
   d. Play Percentages
3. *Advanced Playmaking*
   a. 30-Second Speech
   b. The Image of Leadership
   c. Ruling the Mob

STRATEGIES FOR INDIVIDUALS

The Hook

Let's face it. There is a reason why the hook has survived in songwriting and politics for so long. In music it is usually the catchy part of a song. It's the part of the song that you find yourself singing when you're walking around with your iPod. It's the part that makes you want to listen to it. Sometimes it's the chorus, sometimes it's a quick melody, and in rap it used to be Nate Dawg, Mace, and Little John's lyrics …but not anymore.

To set the hook at a Model UN Conference, a speaker needs to set the tone early with a big first speech. If you have thoroughly researched your topic this will not be a problem. Before the conference, write speeches for the topics discussed in the preparation guides. Practice delivering the speech a few days leading up to the conference using classmates, friends, or the mirror if no other option exists. This early show of force lets the other delegates know that you mean business.

The deepest techniques in the art of The Hook involve the laws of association and *charming, confident* delivery. Your brain is hardwired to memorize repeated experiences. The most advanced delegates wrap their words with Machiavellian force, attaching certain gestures and catch phrases to their speeches. They implant their phrases into your brains and you dream about them at night. Their ideas become associated with their *charm* throughout the rest of the conference. WARNING: This may require **charisma**. (*Review the first two paragraphs on confidence in chapter 2. Do it NOW.*)

Finally avoid being dumb. If your idea is not creative, do not bother talking about it. By setting The Hook early, you can count on second looks by the committee chair and an increase in speaking time.

The Peacock

The Peacock is a strategy we have seen many different delegates attempt to use with varied levels of success. The strategy is easy to do and it works exactly like the bird it is named after. Take one feature of your dress or normal appearance then change it in a pronounced fashion.

One example that comes to mind is of a delegate we once coached in 2004. She never really took much care of her hair during the school year but at Model UN conferences, she made sure that her hair was highlighted and awesome. (*We're guys. We don't really know what you girls do so we're sorry and we can't get into more detail.*) She felt that the fresh cut helped attract attention and it was usually true because she consistently landed a spot on the speakers list early.

Other variations of this strategy can be found in the world of young men's apparel. Some may call this *Rollin' Deep*. We have seen suit jackets and ties. We had the pleasure of coaching another delegate around 2004 that was very similar to The Diplomat delegate. He would always wear the most expensive, colorful silk shirts and ties that he could find. He would start with an advantage in every conference because it would be hard for committee chairs to look past his bright shirts and unmitigated swag.

Mediation

Mediation is a simple strategy that can be used during un-moderated (Un-MOD) caucuses to steal support away from your competition. The tactic is easy enough to employ but it does require a fair measure of showmanship and timing to be effectively executed during competition. If you can successfully identify the critical moment during a debate, this is the strategy for you!

The best place to use the mediation strategy is during Un-MOD. Un-MOD is a portion of every conference where delegates are allowed to promote their ideas and working papers freely and informally. Delegates enjoy this time for a multitude of reasons. They are not constrained by the rules and procedures of the conference so it gives them an opportunity to talk to the other delegates on a more intimate level. Here delegates forge alliances with each other and sow the seeds of goodwill and friendship as diplomats.

Sadly many delegates miss this valuable opportunity to separate themselves from the competition. It is not uncommon for delegates to use this as an opportunity to check their phones, go outside and have a smoke (*yes… I've personally seen it*), or just leave, in general. Not that we need to tell you, but avoid the delegates who demonstrate this reckless behavior.

Dominate Un-MOD by taking control over one of Model UN's most unique phenomena, the "Un-MOD Circle." The Un-MOD Circle is the ring of delegates that usually appears near the front of every conference room. Better delegates attempt to strategically place their circle at the front of the room so that the chair is close enough to overhear their discussions. They think that it will earn them valuable points with the chair. It might help, it might not.

Try this strategy during the beginning of the 1ST Committee Session. The circle will form immediately during the first Un-MOD. It is in its largest and strongest incarnation. You will be somewhere within the circle, speaking and listening. Watch the circle carefully in the beginning and identify those who appear to be the strongest speakers in the room. You will notice how the people nearest to them *gravitate* towards the speakers. Remember that Un-MODS tend to last around five minutes so there's no need to rush into being the loudest voice. Your mission is slightly different than those overeager delegates. Your job is keeping the circle together as it begins to divide. You will use the platform of compromise!

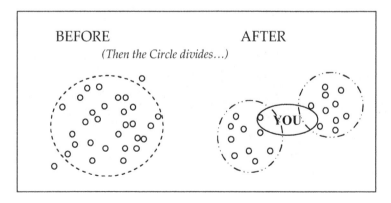

BEFORE   AFTER
(Then the Circle divides…)

Once the circle begins to divide, it is your moment to strike. Dive into the fray and propose a moderate policy solution that responds to the topic. Tell people not to divide yet! Make sure you are loud enough to be heard and don't be afraid to push a little. Many countries will be attracted to someone suggesting a "compromising" and "unified" solution and the chair will be able to witness your Diplomatic skills first hand. It's a win!

UNICEF

This is a clever little trick that we've seen used at several different conferences around the Northeast. The name for this strategy comes from the global child welfare management agency in the United Nations. If you were unaware, UNICEF provides food and supplies for the world's children. It is a noble mission and it should receive much more support. You will dictate the menu and the location of the feeding of the delegates. The food is the care package; you organize the delivery.

The UNICEF strategy attempts to use food to your advantage during the early stages of a Model UN conference. The delivery of this aid parcel isn't meant to purchase support or votes with charitable donations of food. Instead, you are using the feeding ritual as a center for meeting and networking with key players in the committee. This strategy is intended for conferences that last two or more days. It is also more effective in smaller committees.

Remember, you don't have to be the person that buys the food. The best route is to organize an event. It can be as simple as "Hey! Pizza in the Hotel Lobby at 11 PM!" or "Want to get lunch at Applebee's after committee? I love their Asiago Peppercorn Steak!" This tactic has nothing to do with the food, it's an opportunity to create and control a social situation. Get friendly with some of the competition while chewing. Gather useful information. You are also demonstrating leadership with the simple act of organizing an event. People will subconsciously get used to the idea of listening to you. It's a "no lose situation."

There are a few variations of this strategy that we've seen work. Some delegates bring a small candy or gift the first day as a greeting from their nation. It's a nice gesture but we doubt it is going to be a game changer during committee session. We've also witnessed delegates coordinate a pizza delivery with the end of a committee session. This timely "care package" is quick capital to use to win friends and allies.

Advanced Placement
Location! Location! Location! It's an age-old adage in real estate and is useful in MUN as well. The strategy is simple geography.

Make sure you acquire a good seat during the conference. If you're in a flat committee room, you should set up camp two to three rows back near the center. If the room is more like an amphitheater, you should place yourself in the middle of the pack and close to the side. You can stand up from your seat and speak to everyone clearly. Everyone hates arriving early to an event, but you're going to suck it up for the morning session and get there early. As a general rule you should always be aware of your location in relation to the chair and front dais. Stay within eye distance if possible.

There is a laundry list of advantages that accompany this strategy. First, it is easier to get on the speakers list and be recognized for speaking time if you are closer to the chair. Second, good location allows for constant interaction with the front dais—good communication will lead to success. Next, the chair will also be more apt to notice when you are in the process of writing notes or resolutions. If you constantly look busy, you will benefit.

Extend this principle to Un-MOD's as well. During Un-MOD's move any circles that form close to the front dais. Little things like geography can make a difference. Remember the maxim: More visibility means more success!

The Post Master

All seasoned veterans of Model UN know that there are some conferences where speaking time does not come often. For some reason you just can't catch a break. You have great placement in the room and it just doesn't matter. Time passes and your country is never called. You begin to hallucinate from the frustration. You begin to believe that the chair has a secret agenda against you and only you. You tell your advisor, "Look! The chair looked me dead in the eye and just called Sweden. I never get called on. They already called on Sweden 3 times in the last hour." Just when it seems that all hope is lost, you remember that there is still one last chance… with the Post Master strategy.

It is always a good practice at Model UN Conferences to gather contact information from other delegates during the 1st Committee Session. The Post Master strategy depends on strong lines of communication through instant message, notes, texts, and e-mails. Think of it like Twitter. Everyone in the room is a potential "follower" of your tweets! You have to become a reliable information hub, able to relay news and data quickly across a network of people. If you can successfully inform your allies of the status of working papers and other key bits of information, you will succeed. One pitfall: If you're not Teflon Smooth, you may send weird signals when gathering contact information. No one likes a stalker.

The Cheerleader

It's a good habit during any Model UN conference to try and assess the strengths and weaknesses of other delegations. The Cheerleader is a strategy used by delegations that are strong orators (*that's a great SAT word*). For example, when resolutions are presented, this is the ideal moment for the cheerleader to shine.

The lead sponsor is usually the first to speak about the resolution. They may describe major advantages of their solutions yet leave out a few key points that you and your fellow sponsors have determined to be advantageous to the goals of the committee. This is the ideal moment for the cheerleader to emerge from the shadows. As the rhythm of the lead sponsor's monologue approaches a pause, the cheerleader steps in and ignites the committee with their passionate belief in the effects of the presented resolution! (*"De-Fense! *clap *clap De-Fense!"*) Their words are more melodic and dramatic than the objective tone of the sullied presenter. New leadership is now in charge of the committee.

This simple strategy can be employed throughout the course of any committee. When an opposing delegation appears dominant early in a conference, it's in the cheerleader's best interest to join forces with them. The highly visible delegation will present ideas that the committee shows favor towards, but there will be moments where they are looking for vocal support. In order to execute the cheerleader strategy you need to make the most of this short-lived alliance by riding the coattails of your new friend to victory.

The rule of thumb for the cheerleader is that **if the lead delegation says it well, then you say it better.** If the lead delegation speaks to promote a resolution, your delegation will follow them and say it even more persuasively. In order to succeed, this strategy requires a delegate that is a good communicator. The cheerleader does not create her own idea. It is the cheerleader's ability to communicate another's idea that will lead to success.

ac·ro·nym:
[ak-r*uh*-nim]
noun
1. A word formed from the initial letters or groups of letters of words in a set phrase or series of words, as WAC from Women's Army Corps, OPEC from Organization of Petroleum Exporting Countries, or LORAN from Long-Range Navigation.[xiv]

Use this strategy with discretion. Personally, we're not huge fans of acronyms, but we do realize their potential value. If you are able to create a good, witty acronym, it can help your position immensely. Good acronyms are easy to remember and plant seeds in the minds of the audience.

But be warned! The cardinal rule of acronyms: "Don't force it." Over the years we've seen some unique acronyms used in resolutions that were very effective. We have also seen delegates with insubstantial ideas rely on the sole strength of their well-known acronym. They destroyed their chances of winning because they wouldn't abandon the faulty acronym.

One quick hypothetical example of an acronym might be given within a mock World Trade Organization committee. Imagine a specific topic that addresses modern commercial problems, particularly e-commerce. Computer fraud and identity theft are major consumer concerns. A delegation may propose a resolution that includes measures they have dubbed SPAM—Special Pact Against Maliciousness. "Malicious" programs are called viruses, trojans, or spybots. *Spam* is unwanted email. SPAM is a *witty* acronym that, not only accomplishes the desired association with electronic commerce, but also addresses an unwanted electronic "invader." This could work well in committee. It may also fail if the delegation presents poor solutions and refuses to abandon the promoted policy.

STRATEGIES FOR TEAMS

Model UN strategies can change greatly when a school has multiple delegations in the same committee. With multiple delegations, a school can benefit in many different ways. These opposing delegations can work together or fight against each other. This allows for several strategic options with certain tactics leading directly to multiple awards.

Ping Pong

Ping Pong allows a school to take advantage of multiple delegations in the same committee that have strikingly different policies on an issue. Let's imagine that we are watching a committee on Disarmament that includes the United States and the Democratic People's Republic of Korea [DPRK, most commonly known as North Korea]. By sheer happenstance (*or strategic preference*) your school represents both of these nations in the committee. Most schools wouldn't be too excited at the prospect of representing North Korea. True, North Korea's attitude towards human rights and nuclear disarmament are lacking in many areas, but in this disarmament committee we can use these weaknesses as a major advantage.

As advisors, we would have both the US and DPRK push hard at the start of the committee to **polarize** the debate. The Ping Pong strategy (*polarization*) is to divide the room into two opposing sides. The United States will represent the *disarmament* side of the argument while North Korea will argue, "a state's sovereignty will justify the creation of whatever is necessary to defend its border." It is important that **both** delegations lead the different factions of the committee. *The way to establish this leadership is to be the two most vocal opponents against one another.*

Once the two opposing factions (*your school's delegations*) establish their dominance as the leaders of their constituents, it is time to get down to business. Both sides need to push their respective policies in committee—to battle each other like cats and dogs and pass their resolutions. In order for this strategy to succeed, you must be the leader of your faction when the moment of truth arrives. If your voices led to the division of the entire committee and you demonstrated leadership over your bloc, the judges will not have a very difficult decision in rewarding your efforts.

Overwhelm

Have you ever faced overwhelming odds? It is the story of dreams and legends. Maybe you have heard the story of King Leonidas at Thermopylae during the Persian Wars. It is the central story of the movie "300," the loose history of a group of 300 Spartans that were massacred thru a vicious three-day battle against an army of Persians one million strong. In the Overwhelm strategy you are the Persian army of the committee.

The basic premise of Overwhelm is to **acquire as many delegations as possible** and promptly use your huge numerical advantage to dominate a single committee. In this strategy it is important to **be aggressive early**, before your opposition realizes that you have this advantage. A policy must be presented that addresses the intentions of the committee, and your school's member nations will adamantly **push this position**.

With democracy there is great strength in numbers, but only few can be leaders. Though there is certainty in earning an award through Overwhelm-ing a committee, this strategy will require personal sacrifice from the delegations representing weaker nations within your bloc. These delegations may be called upon to yield time to the stronger member states on the speakers list. The simple beauty of this strategy is that the stronger delegations from a school will use its weaker delegations as tools to win a conference. Countries like Djibouti, Sudan, and Azerbaijan will be the weak members whose vote will represent the wave of support for your stronger delegations' resolutions. Yielding time on the speakers list will also help promote the leadership that your group follows.

Though this strategy can almost guarantee a major award, it may also guarantee a loss in team awards. The percentage scoring system used by many conferences around the United States *normalizes* your awards to the number of participants your school has at the conference. This system of scoring punishes schools for taking too many students to a Model United Nations Conference. Whether this is a good or bad idea remains up for debate, but your use of the Overwhelm strategy must take this scoring into consideration if your school is eager to win a team award.

Avoid Crisis

The Avoid Crisis strategy is a major gamble. It is high risk but has the potential for great reward if executed properly. We can personally attest to the effectiveness of the strategy having executed it at HMUN (Harvard) with much success and a second place team award (*Outstanding Large Delegation*).

This strategy begins months before the actual conference with the committee request forms. Your school must **purposely avoid as many crisis committees as possible** and place your best delegates in the Economic and Social Committees (ECOSOC) and General Assembly (GA). With this committee selection you will avoid the best delegates in the conference. Your school's top delegates will be placed in committees where there are many amateur and intermediate participants—many who are far less experienced in *the Dark Arts*. Your most experienced delegates will easily navigate the perils of these committees. Good performances will be rewarded during the closing ceremonies, and since you have "spread the wealth" you are maximizing your school's chances for a team award.

WARNING: Use this strategy with extreme caution. Large committees can be a crapshoot. The best delegates can get lost in these ginormous committee rooms. You have no control over the chair's selections for the speaker's list nor the points or motions on the floor. If your delegation is passed over multiple times, this experimental strategy will quickly turn into a nightmare. There also needs to be a "team" mentality within the group—delegates must be willing to sacrifice personal success for overall team success. The best delegates can be fiercely egotistic and independent so you should already sense this initial difficulty. Advisors (*just like coaches*) need to remind their delegates that it's all about the TEAM! As a delegate, you must put the needs of the team ahead of your own desires.

Play Percentages

This strategy is for team awards. It is pure numbers and hinges upon one limit, the definition of "Large Delegations" and "Small Delegations." To execute your Played Percentages correctly, you must find out the exact number of delegates the conference uses to define their team awards. In the majority of Model UN conferences, team awards are calculated by the number and weight of awards you win divided by the number of delegates you bring. We've been to several conferences where our school has won the vast majority of the individual "best" and "outstanding" awards but have failed to take home a team award. This is the simple math of dividing individual

97

points by 96 delegates instead of our opponent's 24 (*their points were essentially quadrupled*).

In Model United Nations, many committees demand that their delegations practice transparency through its interactions with fellow delegations. The Secretariat, however, is not held to this burden. Percentages for awards are sometimes kept like nuclear secrets, and these cloak and dagger tactics can prove fatal for your school if you miscalculate the total number of delegates that you bring.

At our school we are very driven to earn team awards. Our delegates are constantly estimating conference limits for "large" and "small" delegations. If we are competing for Best Small Delegation, we bring exactly 12–15 delegates to the conference. Most conferences maintain a limit for small delegations to be less than 20. When we bring 19 delegates and the limit is 20, the ratio makes it more difficult to compete for that team award. If your team is aiming to win the Best Large Delegation award, your school needs to stay as close to the dividing line as possible, e.g. if the limit for a small delegation is 20, bring 21 delegates.

ADVANCED PLAYMAKING

Our advanced section is an addition for those delegates seeking the keys to the kingdom. Our language in this section will also be more complex and descriptive because these tactics require the utmost clarity. The social dynamic that takes place among powerful personalities is clearly different than the mundane flow of banter between the average pedestrian and a fellow bystander. Powerful personalities act with intention and purpose (*remember the* goal-oriented mindset *discussed in Chapter 2*). Most people do not focus on the outcome of their conversations with others, but **powerful people always have a goal in mind.** When you encounter these people in Model UN, they are usually in the process of administering a strategic plan to steer the opinions of their allies, the chair, and the committee in their favor. This is the *manipulative* form of diplomacy evidenced by this quote from political journalist David Frost, "Diplomacy is the art of letting someone else have your way."

The timbre of the conversations between powerful personalities is very concentrated and intense. Goal-oriented communicators are very aware of the words and body language of the other participants. They are scoping for nervousness, lies, and vulnerabilities. There are some very honest people with good intentions who will do their best to assuage the fears of delegates who have a vested interest in the subject of debate, but there are also manipulative marauders who seek personal gain through the guise of diplomatic verbosity. Regardless of the audience, you must exercise extreme awareness and maintain your own sense of purpose throughout this dialogue.

The 30-Second Speech

In large and small committees, there are small windows of opportunity to say something very substantial in 30 seconds or less. There is usually a great power underlying these moments. Your words can be pivotal as they often are the prelude to voting procedures.

When analyzing the motivation of voting and other forms of decision-making, we must be extremely objective if we are to adopt a strategy that provides the greatest means to our end. In political science and economic theory, there is a model called the Self-Interested Voter Hypothesis (SIVH). You may initially argue that this is Model UN and delegates must stay "on policy," but the resolutions that appear in committee are usually positioned as pillars of compromise, promoting an alternative hypothesis of Group-Interested Voting.

We will quickly employ the dialectical strategy from Chapter 5: *both hypotheses are more or less true.* Further, there is a deeper foundation for people's reactions that underlies both of these models of voter behavior: **emotion**. This is the axis about which you must spin your speech.

There is an innate human ability called **empathy**. It is our ability to feel another person's emotions. Empathy is triggered when you observe another person experiencing his or her own powerful emotions. If you have ever seen a movie that made you sad or happy, it is most likely because a character in the movie had suffered a loss or gained a victory of some sort. It makes you *react*. This is what you hope to achieve with your 30-second speech.

To begin, take a moment to emotionally assess the potential "tragedy" that will occur if your plan is not accepted by the committee (*yes, it's a simulation... but you have to passionately describe the humanity of the situation; don't go to the point of apocalypse, but express the "tragic" consequences*). **Like an actor, you have to embrace the role of the Hero* in this possible calamity and convey to the audience that they can be Heroes, too.** You can experiment with the level of drama that you add to the role, but it cannot be absent from your speech. There needs

---

* If you are interested in storytelling, mythology, or existentialism, the archetype of the *Hero* is very well described by Joseph Campbell.

to be enough emotion so that the committee *feels* your feelings about the issue. The issue must *feel* important.

So here's a quick recipe. **First**, sum up the historical story in one or two sentences *in human terms*; political terms have no weight, instead you must personalize the hardship and sadness that has happened or will happen in the future. **Second**, you describe with one or two sentences the hopefulness and beauty of the changes that can occur if the committee takes action. Again, you must say this *in human terms*, NOT political, newsworthy hyperbole. This may sound cliché but when you ask for help from a place of vulnerability and love, nearly all human beings will answer your call.

Rules: Do not rush this speech. Insert thoughtful pauses. Make strong eye contact. Feel the emotion of the hardship in the first statement, and feel the emotion of the hope in the second statement. When you are finished, take an extra few seconds to stand there and look at the committee, demonstrating your trust in them and vulnerability to their actions. Then thank the chair.

One last trick can be included here, and it may require a little creativity. Over the course of committee, there will be a memorable phrase or joke that caught everyone's attention. If you can find a way to work that into your speech, you will touch their emotions AND their humor.

The Image of Leadership

The opposition can be pushy and forceful and require you to step up your game. To the contrary, you may encounter delegates who are far too relaxed for a crisis and, somehow, they end up as your toughest opponent. Your behavior must adapt to the competition.

101

You must be efficient and communicate clearly. You must demand respect and give respect. It may not be obvious, but the image of leadership, first and foremost, refers to the respect you have earned from everyone else in the room.

Though you may be looking for some clear formula to accomplish this, there is no such thing. Earning the respect of 20 people might require 20 different strategies. Politicians carefully craft their speeches for each event. In committee you will be expected to graciously meet strangers, introduce yourself to the chair, smile through difficulty, look good, plan ahead, speak well, etc. To these ends, it is imperative that you constantly exercise the skills we gave to you in Chapters 2 and 3. Those techniques are the foundation for the appearance of leadership. Foresight, communication, and respect are the capstones that bring those skills to the upper echelon of diplomatic action.

In general, we will attempt to chart a course for you in the following paragraphs. Before committee begins, you should have met a few people who you will be competing against. Be personal with them. Consider these people resources and demonstrate to them that you can be their resource as well. You should meet the chair, too. One possible reason to talk to the chair is to ask them a question about the background guide or some current event that is directly related to the topics of committee. If you're using the proper body language and eye contact, other delegates will notice your interactions and put you on their "radar."

As speeches begin scan the room for regional alliances, send out some notes to the strong delegates who have similar positions, and begin forming your bloc with weaker delegates who are looking for a strong alliance. **Go** through the proper courtesy of a personal introduction, and a statement of their goals within committee. Keep expanding your bloc, inviting other delegates and **taking them through this protocol** while keeping tabs on the other strong delegates, but do not engage those stronger delegates in debate until it is ultimately necessary. If a strong delegate comes into your circle forcibly, stop them and demand that they relax. Tell this *gavel hunter* to introduce him or her self and demand that they **follow the protocol of introducing themselves and stating their goals in committee** (*we're bolding this because it is a very strong tactic for keeping up your appearance as a leader*). You are the enforcer; you are demonstrating that mutual respect will be maintained among the contributors to your bloc. If this new delegate is giving ideas that have already been offered, stop them and point to the people who have already contributed these ideas. If the power delegate offers nothing new, tell them that you are unwilling to include them in your bloc. Be nice about it and send them elsewhere, even if they come from a P5 country. You wanted to be a leader, right? Well, being a good leader implies that eventually you will have to tell people "No." Besides, why invite the Russian Federation into your alliance if you know that they *might* end up taking *all* of the credit? You are not the only delegation who is jealous of the lucky delegate who was gifted with a powerful country. And you can use that camaraderie to your advantage when the resolutions come to a vote. Most people enjoy routing for the underdog.

As resolutions become the game, outline the topics and clauses and gather your bloc to mutually plan the document. Each person should have something to write and you should create some digital archive like a shared folder in Dropbox or Google Drive. Ask the chair if they have a preference for how the document should be prepared (*this is another opportunity to talk to the chair and show your leadership*). If any member of the bloc takes too much ownership of the resolution, do not hesitate to talk to the rest of your allies about it. When it is time for questions and answers, keep up the same agreement and mutual respect that went into the document. Let each defendant answer about the part of the resolution that they wrote and keep eye contact with them as they answer questions. If they are not sufficiently detailed, you will be able to read it in their face and expression and react immediately by filling in the details. Place yourself between any other power delegates and your fellow allies so that you are more aware of the awkward pauses that require another voice.

Maintaining the image of leadership is a long-term mission. It requires persistence and constant awareness of your audience. It also requires your careful handling of the other power delegates in your committee. Do not overly stress yourself out about your appearance among the masses. At the end of the day, it is only a simulation. As Samuel Smiles said, "We learn wisdom from failure much more than from success. We often discover what will do, by finding out what will not do; and probably he who never made a mistake never made a discovery."

Controlling The Mob

Without a doubt, this is the most difficult task to accomplish. On one hand, you should not assume that there is actually a way to "control" the mob. On the other hand, you should have the faith that they can be "steered" in alternative directions.

The mob operates on simple rules. You can think of it like a baby. Flashy lights, loud noises, and surprises can snap the crowd to attention. Fear from danger can cause a sudden flight or evacuation. A challenge or demand can cause a temper tantrum, also known as a riot. As you can see, the crowd is a lot like a big baby.

You cannot control this baby; you can only hope to appease it. Sometimes you will have to clap your hands and excite your intended emotion. Other times you may have to shout above the crowd with a strange accent to create some humor and bring their attention back to your intention. There will be moments of utter chaos; you will have to get in the middle and start dictating the flow of information like a teacher or a drill sergeant (*see the "clipboard technique" in Chapter 10*). When the crowd is in shambles, you must have a battle cry to bring them back together.

Whenever you use any of these techniques, you must act like the star of the show. Remember we told you that the baby likes shiny, flashy lights and loud noises. You have to be that glittery object of fascination if you hope to be noticed by an unruly crowd. If you know any gymnastics tricks or maybe you have a good singing voice, you can use them here. You can also throw some change on a hard floor to make the elongated metallic, clingy noise of money (*then you can make a joke like, "do you see how much money I have invested in this resolution?!"*). Yes, these are ridiculous tactics. Amazingly, they will work. This is stupid, simple crowd control.

To sum this last segment up, the crowd's actions are indicative of their collective emotion. You must be the rationality that guides this untamable force. You cannot control emotion; you can only guide it or startle it from its current path. We apologize if these instructions are not explicit enough, but we can only provide a general metaphor.

"Nice Kimono Dawg"
by Thomas White

CHAPTER 7: Dressed for Success

Winning... and looking so damn good while doing it

When dressing for a Model UN conference it is your job to appear professional. Common sense would dictate appropriate attire is necessary for the conference if you want to win. Essentially, it means that your clothes and style must not be a distraction. So gentlemen, go out and get a nice pair of slacks, and a button down shirt with a matching tie. Ladies: think Hillary Clinton. A snappy business suit with a conservative blouse will project a winning image. Furthermore, sneakers are for gym class. Wear your best dress shoes. This chapter will include photos and specific examples because we've been to many conferences and witnessed many poor choices of attire.

There are rules for dressing *appropriately*, but there are tricks to dressing *well*. As we progress through this chapter we will help you understand the ways to look presentable to the committee and maintain the respect of your chair at first glance. It is your job to appear professional and serious. Spiked collars and fishnet stockings do not win respect in professional environments.

Before we dive into the pertinent details of "Western Business Attire," we want to take a moment to apologize to our audience. We are deeply sorry that the rules are slightly worse for women than for men. We don't believe that this policy is morally right and we firmly believe in women's rights, but unfortunately society as a whole hasn't proven to be so forgiving.

As a diplomat it is important to realize that some cultures do not value the same freedoms that are available in the United States. There are places in the world where women can be physically abused and beaten for revealing any skin beyond their eyes and hands. This is just one more reason why an institution like the United Nations is so important for the world.

Ladies, when you're packing your suitcase and picking out your skirts for the Model UN conference, think about the rest of the world for a moment and respectfully choose a few skirts that are a bit longer. International delegates are attending conferences much more often. Some of these international delegates are extremely confused by the attire of other young women at these conferences. In an extreme case, what they deem as provocative attire can be emotionally traumatizing to them. It is the truth. Accept it and respect their social norms. It shows that you are a respectful, diplomatic person.

The rules for male attire are simple and straightforward. Suits haven't changed much since the United Nations was founded. Shoes should match the belt, colors should be muted and appear natural. Ties and single-color button-down shirts are the typical attire for male delegates. Though this should be obvious, we still witness many ridiculous outfits. Overall, you should choose apparel that represents you as a sophisticated, professional individual. This does not only apply to Model UN, but it also applies to life.

The Contents of this Chapter Include:
1. *Women's attire*
2. *Men's attire*
3. *The finer details*

WOMEN'S ATTIRE

We'll start with women because this is an instructional book and as far as attire is concerned, women break most of the rules. We have the courtesy of overhearing the advisors of other schools, especially international schools, who voice their **strong concerns** about the way young women are dressing at <u>ALL</u> of these conferences. We will say this once more: if you are a young woman and you care about the way you look, save the short skirts and lacy stockings for the dance. **They are inappropriate.** Britney Spears *doesn't* participate in Model UN.

Our discussion of women's attire will begin with a demonstration of "appropriate western business attire." On the next page you'll find a picture of six women who are dressed well, but would probably be better suited for the workplace. We are using this picture because there are some "do's and don'ts" that can be highlighted by the outfits shown.

A   B   C   D   E   F

First off, all of these outfits would easily pass as "professional attire," but there are some examples here that are treading on the edge of "inappropriate" for a Model UN conference. **A** is wearing a skirt that is a bit too tight and a *slight* bit too short. As a woman in a skirt, you need to be sure that sitting and crossing your legs doesn't require constant adjustment. If you keep grabbing the bottom of your skirt and pushing it down from the simple action of sitting and standing, your skirt is too short.

The woman on the far right, **F**, is also pushing an edge. She is wearing a halter top that shows all of her shoulders. This would be fine for a casual business atmosphere and a semiformal event, but this is still too casual for a MUN conference. **C** and **D** are also dressed a little too casual. Both of these women would look more professional in a women's suit jacket.

It is important to dress for your body shape. We all have parts of our bodies that can look awkward in clothes that are not chosen wisely. If a man is very short, it is very foolish for him to wear a tie that is too long. When a woman is very tall, five-inch heels can make her look like a giant; those shoes would be a poor choice.

Another nuance that women need to be aware of: with professional attire, you should make yourself **look attractive but without "aiming for sexy."** Any sort of attire that is intentionally provocative or accentuates the body in an obviously sexual way ceases to be attractive and becomes *a distraction*. **A** is wearing a full-body skirt that is almost skin tight. This is definitely inappropriate for MUN. **E** is wearing a very nice dress that is very feminine and not pushing any boundaries. If the cut across her torso was lower, then there might be a problem.

The women in this photo are not wearing any accessories other than the necklace in **C** and the belts on **A** and **F**. Accessories are the key to being noticed. Certain accessories are designed to catch your eye. When you wear an adornment that stands out, you are "peacocking." We've already written about this strategy in the previous chapter.

Try to avoid any clothing or fashion decisions that could be considered suggestive. You need to be aware of every detail of your dress including stockings. They should not be fishnet, cross-hatched, or lacy. Your V-neck should never show portions of your bra. Your makeup should be light and well blended. Your lipstick should not be blood-red or overly sparkly. Save the glitter for arts and crafts.

The shoes that the women in the photo are wearing are acceptable. Many young women at MUN conferences are wearing very high heels. We don't think that high heels are inappropriate, but the young women who wear 4-inch heels are definitely stretching the rules. The higher the heel, the closer it comes to inappropriate. Super high heels are a distraction. In addition if you don't wear high heels normally, practice wearing them before the conference. You do not want to walk like an injured giraffe when you make your entrance into the committee room.

Here are a few tricks to try and integrate into your wardrobe during a Model UN conference. Your nail polish can be your way of **peacocking**. It is a low risk attention getter when choosing a bright color for your nails. A clinking bracelet can call for subtle attention as long as you don't make it overtly loud. Your hair is not an issue unless you totally neglect it. Final point:

"ALWAYS BE CLASSY."

The women in the previous picture are wearing clothes that are almost perfect. The only one that is pushing a boundary is the woman on the right. Her skirt is a *little* too short and *slightly* too tight. If you search "Women's Business Attire" on Google images, every skirt in the first 100 photos goes to the knees.

Here's a more timely set of modern, teenage examples: a picture that is very similar to what girls are wearing today:

The first two girls on the left are appropriately dressed. The three girls to the right are wearing skirts that are too short and heels that are too high (*which is much worse in combination*). They look like they're dressed more for a sweet sixteen than an international conference.

MEN'S ATTIRE

There aren't too many rules for a man's attire at a Model UN conference. Therefore, men are less likely to break the rules of proper dress attire. All men, regardless of age, are held to the same beliefs when it comes to professional dress. Men *cannot* stretch the boundaries anywhere near as much as women because their options are limited; pants or shorts, shoes or sneakers, short sleeve or long sleeve, jacket or no jacket, it's pretty boring overall. But, we'll do our best to provide you with some options to aid you at the conference. If you dress well, you'll win people's respect immediately.

One thing is certain. If you'd like to know whether you are dressed well, you should ask a woman. According to women, the major difference between a well-dressed man and a poorly dressed man is how well the man's clothes <u>fit</u>. If a man's clothes *fit* him well, he is considered to *dress* well. A well-dressed man wears clothes that FIT him; the sleeve falls slightly beyond the wrist, the pants have the perfect "break" 6 inches above the ankle, and his shoulders fill the jacket comfortably.

| A | B | C | D | E | F |

Although these are adult men, the rules are no different for them than they are for you. Model **A** should stand out since he does not fit the MUN definition of western business attire. He's not dressed appropriately for a Model UN conference because he lacks a shirt and tie.

Instead, it looks like he's going to a family birthday party. D is wearing too much black and his shirt does not have a collar or a tie. He might be able to pull it off with a forgiving chair, but he's crossing a *boundary*. He should have a tie and a button-down shirt. Everyone else looks just fine, BUT... **B** and **F** are wearing clothes that **fit well**. **C**, although he's a small guy, he seems to be wearing clothes that are far too big for him. **E** might be wearing pants that are *slightly* too baggy as well.

Finer points: Wear a shirt with some color. You can wear any color that stands out. If you feel uncomfortable, wear a crazy colored tie (*these are ways to* **peacock**). Make sure the color of your leather shoes is the same as the color of your leather belt. Do not wear sneakers. Do *something* with your hair. (*You can even do a fauxhawk if you want. We had a student win his only award ever, a gavel, when he did a fauxhawk and put silver in his hair. That was the Model UN epitome of peacocking.*)

THE FINER DETAILS:

PACKING YOUR BAG

This is a simple list of things to bring with you. They require very little explanation.
-Toothbrush & Toothpaste
-Deodorant
-Hair stuff (*gel, mousse, hair spray, shampoo, conditioner... whatever*)
-Your own soap if you're picky
-Razor& Shaving Cream
-Light cologne or perfume (*don't overdo it... disgusting*)
-Five pairs of underwear
-Notebook, pens, and a small pad for notes
-Laptop if you're writing or if you're allowed
-Accessories for clothing

PLEASE... Remember to shower every day. Personal hygiene is paramount to success.

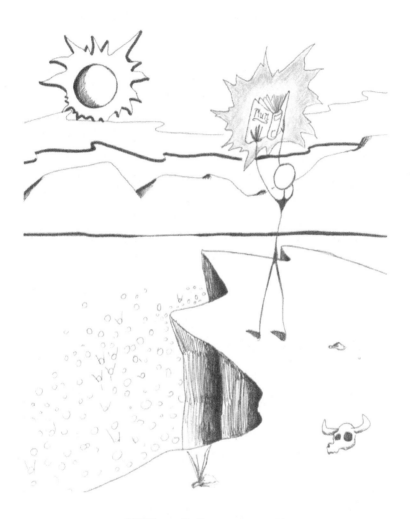

"The Message"
by Thomas White

CHAPTER 8: Expository Writing

Position Papers, Working Papers, and Resolutions... Oh My...

Writing is EXTREMELY important. **You will only get better at writing by writing!** For many students this task is daunting because of either a lack of practice or an unawareness of the process that accompanies it. You, however, are going to be willing to make that sacrifice and write more to improve this vital skill.

To aid in your writing you must read as much as possible. Start by finding a great book that truly *interests* you. After completing several books within your comfort zone, don't be afraid to branch out and challenge yourself with less familiar topics. Regardless of the topic, you can learn an author's writing style simply by reading his or her works. This will also help to improve your vocabulary and observe the way that sentences are linked together to make effective arguments.

Persuasive writing is a style unto itself. It is the method in which you project your view to a specific audience. During this chapter we will explore the way to address your audience and how to write with a purpose in mind.

The Contents of this Chapter Include:
1. *Essential Practices for MUN writing*
2. *Position Papers*
3. *Working Papers and Resolutions*

Essential Practices for MUN Writing

Don't be overly sensitive to criticism of your writing. All good writers have their work scrutinized by any number of critics. There are some who are able to articulate their opinions with ease. For most, the arduous task of writing is a handicap to their creativity. Others who can express their views verbally may not be able to transfer those opinions to the page. For all writers, the process of writing is the same. Ideas must be generated, revised and edited before being published.

In Model UN, you have to make **arguments**. An argument is meant to persuade the audience that a person's opinion is correct. Use elections as an example. Every politician makes an **argument** *for* or *against* certain policies. A politician's choice about *right* and *wrong* is described as their **position**. This position is presented to sway public opinion on particular issues in the favor of the speaker.

Delegates during a Model UN conference are forced to create a "position" as well. Before a conference begins, delegates write about **WHY** the policy of a nation is the **BEST** and most effective solution to a conflict. These position papers are reviewed by staff members from the committee and occasionally included in the scoring.

To make a long story short, abandon what you think you know about your creative abilities in writing a paper. You need to write clearly and concisely with no fluff. You do not express your personal emotions ever!

We came up with some rules for writing position papers. The first two rules will be introduced from the perspective of the writing you're supposed to do in science class because there is a great deal of similarities. Typically, your science teacher may talk about writing in the "third person passive."

Third Person Passive:

"Approximately 50 milliliters of liquid were poured and measured with a 100-milliliter graduated cylinder. The meniscus was recorded off at 50.4 milliliters."

First Person Active:

"I poured about 50 mL of water into the cylinder with the lines and my partner measured the height of the water in it. It was hard to see the meniscus. Many errors could've been messed up."

This type of "lab report" writing is a great analogy for the difference between good and bad writing in Model UN. The bad science paper is written in first person with several vague descriptive words. There is a sentence where the author writes about what the lab group didthen there is another sentence about the author's feelings. Your science teacher will find many problems with the second example while finding the first example acceptable. In Model UN your writing must be very different from English class writing, just like your science reports must be simple and clear (*yet horribly boring*). Model UN requires the same 'boring' writing. These next two rules are a result of this comparison.

4 Important Rules for Writing in MUN

Rule 1: All working papers and resolutions should be written *predominantly* in the third person. (Like science class)

Rule 2: If any emotional adjectives and actions are ever stated, they must be written as if you are speaking on behalf of the people you represent, i.e. "We as a people," "Our nation," "The state of Djibouti…"

These two rules seem to be in conflict with one another. They are your two basic "frames" from which to write your paper. Realize the only exception to Rule 1 is Rule 2.

When you write a paper in Model UN, you typically start by writing from the frame of Rule 1. In your paper, most of your arguments should start with a statement that describes a situation from the third person point of view. As your statement develops into a policy that your delegation supports, you must begin to apply the second rule and use more first person statements, speaking and identifying as a plural version of the country or department that you represent.

Here are two simple examples of the balance between these two rules. The first example is balanced. The second example is a poor attempt to satisfy the balance between these two rules.

Obeys first two rules: "The health of the people of Africa is in dire straits. Outbreaks of Ebola are a yearly occurrence, two million children younger than five are dying from malaria each year, and HIV currently infects more than twenty million people. This health crisis is imperative to the nation of Uganda as we are confronting the decimation of the health of our people. Our fate is tied to our neighbors and the world's progress is tied to the fate of Africa."

A poor version of this paragraph: "The health of Africa has been getting worse. Every year we see Ebola break out in an African country. Two million of our children are sadly dying before they turn five. 20 million HIV and AIDS patients are dying. As Uganda, I believe that our health is so poor because the rest of Africa is also suffering so badly. We will fight for the health of Africa as the Ugandan delegate in the WHO."

The differences in these two paragraphs are stark. The second paragraph is far too 'personal.' The person uses "I," they use the words "sadly" and "badly," and they declare that they will fight. The whole opinion sounds relatively informal when compared to the first paragraph. In the first paragraph, the final two sentences use the words "we" and "our" but they are speaking as a nation, not as an individual.

As a delegate, you are a representative of MANY PEOPLE. When writing as a *delegate of a nation*, your opinion must be the opinion of the entire nation. You are not allowed to have a "personal" opinion.

Rule 3: Your language must be **action-oriented**.

This is another difficult concept for an inexperienced writer. The action-oriented mindset deals with "actions." Where you may have written phrases like "Uganda wants to," you now have to write phrases like "Uganda *will*." For example:

"Uganda **will** advance the concept of an African Center for Disease Control. The ACDC **will** serve two roles. It **will** function as a health data plexus, managing statistical studies of the past, present, and future. It **will** also serve as a control center for the multitudes of healthcare solutions that are permeating the entire continent. While filling these two roles, the ACDC **will** increase..."

We know the word "will" is being repeated over and over. Believe it or not, that's appropriate for the ONE paragraph in which you promote your ACTIONS. Use the word "will" just like we used the word "will;" over and over again.[xv]

Rule 4: PROOFREAD! And again... and again...

This should be a rule for life, no matter what sort of writing you're doing (*even in* **texting,** *as well as* **emails** *to friends*). If you feel that proofreading your writing is unnecessary, you're wrong. It is one of the most important steps of the process and can't be overlooked.

Position Papers

Awards have been lost because of poor position papers. As we've already described, you need to know the definition of a position. In a position paper, you have to state 'Who, What, When, and Where...' but the *really* important parts are *How and Why*. You must convince the reader that you are taking the *most appropriate* **actions** about the *most important* **issues.** Your position is a statement of your goals for the entire committee. You can make those goals about one or two major policy changes that you'd like to promote, but try not to exceed that number. If you feel that your paper is too short with two major proposed policies, you have a few options. First, you need to do more research. Then you can:

1. Write another paragraph to better introduce the situation that you'd like to improve.

OR

2. Write another paragraph about the UN's goals and how an improvement in this situation will advance those goals.

Facts and statistics are also vital to a position paper. Stating them should be done in the third person and in a straightforward manner. Yes, this may sound like you are stating things that people already know. It's OK. You'll be listing facts and citing research word-for-word; then you will restate that your position is based on those facts.

Lastly, you will say how your policies **will** meet the goals of the United Nations.

We're going to give you a quick formula for starting your first draft of the position paper. You should do steps 1, 2, and 3 at least one month before the committee. The later steps need to be done before you hand in the paper.

Step 1: Read the background guide and read Appendix B. Follow our directions in the appendix for researching your topic. When you get to step 4 of that research, you should then start your position paper.

Step 2: Make sure you follow the format requested by your chair in the background guide. If the format is not given, it is safe to use the following: size 12 font, Garamond font style, 1.5 line spacing, and 1-inch margins. The top of your paper should have *your country* listed first, followed by the *committee*, the *topic(s)* in your paper, your *school*, and finally your names. These should be on the left side of the paper without any sort of numbering or bullets.

Step 3: Write your introduction. Do exactly A, B, C, & D, in order.
   (A) It should consist of one or two initial statements about a major issue from the background guide for which you wish to suggest a corrective policy.
   (B) The next two or three sentences should consist of facts used to reinforce the importance of this issue.

(C) The following sentences describe what effects the situation is having on your country or how your country can help with the situation because it has successfully solved or prevented this problem.

(D) The last sentence or two should be a small summary of the actions that you think can combat this predicament and advance the goals of the United Nations.

Step 4: Now, write one or two full paragraphs about each of these four topics—A, B, C, and D. If you suggest more than one major change in policy, you should have at least two paragraphs for D.

Step 5: Proofread. Give it to a friend and have them proofread, too. Ask your history teacher if your writing is clear. Keep your eye out for news articles and more statistics. Continue researching.

Step 6: Put more proof into your position paper. Rewrite a few sentences that can be made better. Use the thesaurus for a *few* words that you think can make it sound smarter (*Don't do this too much...we can usually see when you overexploit the thesaurus*).

Step 7: Proofread, proofread. Then proofread it one more time.

Step 8: Proofread it some more.

Working Papers and Resolutions

Let's get this "working paper vs. resolution" discussion settled. They are essentially the same thing. A working paper is only called a resolution AFTER the rest of the room votes and the working paper PASSES as a "resolution." Technically, all "resolutions" were once called "working papers" because they had to be developed and written in order to be presented for a vote. Since the goal is always to pass your resolution, we are going to call all working papers "resolutions."

Resolutions are slightly easier to write than position papers. All resolutions are written according to this basic process:

1. Issues will be raised in committee and you will write these down as "preambulatory clauses."

2. Solutions to solve these issues will be discussed in committee and amongst your coterie of 'allies.' These solutions will be written down very specifically as "operative clauses."

3. You now discuss your resolution with fellow delegations or "sponsors" that may agree to add and/or edit content for your resolution. Then you campaign for allies who will agree that your solutions are truly a representation of a consensus view, and you ask them to support you as "signatories."

All three of these steps will be happening simultaneously throughout committee. Your delegation can choose to attack them in any order, but rest assured, all three of these directives MUST be successful in order for you to pass a resolution.

There is a specific format for resolutions that can be found in every Model UN preparation guide. These preparation guides are given in nearly every conference on the planet. At the top of the page, on the left side, you will be expected to write the following things in this order:

(a) The Committee
(b) The Topic
(c) The Sponsors (hopefully your delegation will be first)
(d) The Signatories

There are always multiple sponsors and signatories. Most conferences have adopted a policy that the list of sponsors and signatories should be alphabetized. If the secretariat of the conference hasn't adopted this policy, you should aim to have your delegation named first.

As there are multiple sponsors, you should expect that you would never write a resolution on your own. The moment you start suggesting solutions to the issues in committee, you should be suggesting collective political actions. Once you begin writing them into your proposed resolutions as "operative clauses," other delegations will offer more suggestions about the content of your resolution.[xvi]

After the aforementioned list, the layout of the content of a resolution begins with a declaration of the committee you are representing, e.g. "The General Assembly," or "The Security Council," (including the comma). Following this declaration, there are only two parts left to the resolution and they occur in this order: a series of *preambulatory* clauses followed by a series of action or *operative* clauses.[xvii]The preambulatory clauses are a detailed account of the issues that necessitate the actions that will be declared in your resolution. The operative clauses are a detailed account of the **collective** political actions that the General Assembly [GA] agrees to take (assuming the committee has voted to pass your resolution).

Preambulatory Clauses

Preambulatory clauses are very simple. The background guides of most GAs outline the issues that are important for your committee to discuss. Your preambulatory clauses are a list of sentences describing these issues and the past actions that have addressed these issues. It is rare to see a preamble that highlights previous resolutions or international policies that have succeeded or failed. *Your preambulatory clauses are much more effective when you highlight past international actions!*

Each sentence in the preamble's list of clauses has a slight twist to the format. The first phrase of each sentence must come from the following list of phrases:

Affirming	Expressing its appreciation	Noting with regret
Alarmed by	Expressing its satisfaction	Noting with deep concern
Approving	Fulfilling	Noting with satisfaction
Aware of	Fully alarmed	Noting further
Bearing in mind	Fully aware	Noting with approval
Believing	Fully believing	Observing
Confident	Further deploring	Reaffirming
Contemplating	Further recalling	Realizing
Convinced	Guided by	Recalling
Declaring	Having adopted	Recognizing
Deeply concerned	Having considered	Referring
Deeply conscious	Having considered further	Seeking
Deeply convinced	Having devoted attention	Taking into account
Deeply disturbed	Having examined	Taking into consideration
Deeply regretting	Having heard	Taking note
Desiring	Having received	Viewing with
Emphasizing	Having studied	appreciation
Expecting	Keeping in mind	Welcoming

The following excerpt is a list of the preambulatory clauses from UN Resolution 242, written in 1967:

Expressing its continuing concern with the grave situation in the Middle East,

Emphasizing the inadmissibility of the acquisition of territory by war and the need to work for a just and lasting peace in which every State in the area can live in security,

Emphasizing further that all Member States in their acceptance of the Charter of the United Nations have undertaken a commitment to act in accordance with Article 2 of the Charter,

There are two details to discuss here. First, **every** clause ends with a comma (even the last one). Second, two of these are very *qualitative* statements. The third clause is the only one that specifically cites a factual Historical event or document. This is acceptable.

Most of the preambles you will read in conference resolutions are much longer and more detailed than is necessary. You should strive for simplicity while recognizing that there are many delegates that would like to include *anything* in your resolution. There is a fine balance between being as concise as possible while also allowing other delegates to make suggestions. Achieving this balance will be the biggest difficulty for any delegate who attempts to be the lead sponsor for a resolution.

Operative Clauses

Operative clauses immediately follow the list of preambulatory clauses. They are always in the form of a numbered outline. Sometimes there is a bulleted list that accompanies a numbered statement. The entire set of operative clauses is a list of statements that describe the committee's planned actions to solve the issues described by the preambulatory clauses.

Like the preambulatory clauses, each operative clause must begin with a word or phrase that comes from the list below:

Accepts	Endorses	Further requests
Affirms	Expresses its appreciation	Further resolves
Approves	Expresses its hope	Has resolved
Authorizes	Further invites	Notes
Calls	Deplores	Proclaims
Calls upon	Designates	Reaffirms
Condemns	Draws the attention	Recommends
Confirms	Emphasizes	Regrets
Congratulates	Encourages	Reminds
Considers	Endorses	Requests
Declares accordingly	Expresses its appreciation	Solemnly affirms
Deplores	Expresses its hope	Strongly condemns
Designates	Further invites	Supports
Draws the attention	Further proclaims	Takes note of
Emphasizes	Further reminds	Transmits
Encourages	Further recommends	Trusts

The following examples of operative clauses are also taken from UN Resolution 242:

1. *Affirms* that the fulfillment of Charter principles requires the establishment of a just and lasting peace in the Middle East which should include the application of both the following principles:
   - Withdrawal of Israeli armed forces from territories occupied in the recent conflict;
   - Termination of all claims or states of belligerency and respect for and acknowledgement of the sovereignty, territorial integrity and political independence of every State in the area and their right to live in peace within secure and recognized boundaries free from threats or acts of force;

2. *Affirms* further the necessity
   - For guaranteeing freedom of navigation through international waterways in the area;
   - For achieving a just settlement of the refugee problem;
   - For guaranteeing the territorial inviolability and political independence of every State in the area, through measures including the establishment of demilitarized zones;

135

3. *Requests* the Secretary General to designate a Special Representative to proceed to the Middle East to establish and maintain contacts with the States concerned in order to promote agreement and assist efforts to achieve a peaceful and accepted settlement in accordance with the provisions and principles in this resolution;

4. *Requests* the Secretary-General to report to the Security Council on the progress of the efforts of the Special Representative as soon as possible.

Again, let's take note of two details. First, each operative clause is finished with a semi-colon except for the final clause that is concluded with a period. Second, these clauses are VERY SPECIFIC. Should you be less specific with your own resolutions, it will be very difficult for you to win the alliance of co-sponsors and signatories.

We will conclude this chapter with one more UN resolution for you to take a look at. As you proofread your own resolutions in the future, you should compare and contrast your writing to the writing contained in current UN resolutions (specifics, specifics!). UN resolutions can be found easily with a simple Google search. You can also search the United Nations websites (Start here: http://www.unsystem.org/ and then connect to the individual committee's websites. Type "resolution" into the first search box you see!).

64/297. The United Nations Global Counter-Terrorism Strategy
The General Assembly,

Reaffirming the United Nations Global Counter-Terrorism Strategy, contained in General Assembly resolution 60/288 of 8 September 2006, and recalling Assembly resolution 62/272 of 5 September 2008, which called for, inter alia, an examination in two years of progress made in the implementation of the Strategy and for consideration to be given to updating it to respond to changes, as provided for in those resolutions,

Recalling its resolution 64/235 of 24 December 2009 on the institutionalization of the Counter-Terrorism Implementation Task Force,

Also recalling the pivotal role of the General Assembly in following up the implementation and the updating of the Strategy,

Renewing its unwavering commitment to strengthening international cooperation to prevent and combat terrorism in all its forms and manifestations,

Recognizing that international cooperation and any measures undertaken by Member States to prevent and combat terrorism must fully comply with their obligations under international law, including the Charter of the United Nations, in particular the purposes and principles thereof, and relevant international conventions and protocols, in particular human rights law, refugee law and international humanitarian law,

Convinced that the General Assembly is the competent organ, with universal membership, to address the issue of international terrorism,

Mindful of the need to enhance the role of the United Nations and the specialized agencies, within their mandates, in the implementation of the Strategy,

Underlining the fact that the Counter-Terrorism Implementation Task Force should continue to carry out its activities within the framework of its mandate, with policy guidance offered by Member States through interaction with the General Assembly on a regular basis,

1. *Reiterates its strong and unequivocal condemnation* of terrorism in all its forms and manifestations, committed by whomever, wherever and for whatever purposes, as it constitutes one of the most serious threats to international peace and security;
2. *Reaffirms* the United Nations Global Counter-Terrorism Strategy and its four pillars, which constitute an ongoing effort, and calls upon Member States, the United Nations and other appropriate international, regional and subregional organizations to step up their efforts to implement the Strategy in an integrated manner and in all its aspects;
3. *Takes note* of the report of the Secretary-General entitled

"United Nations Global Counter-Terrorism Strategy: activities of the United Nations system in implementing the Strategy";

4. *Also takes note* of the measures that Member States and relevant international, regional and subregional organizations have adopted within the framework of the Strategy, as presented in the report of the Secretary-General and at the second biennial review of the Strategy, on 8 September 2010, all of which strengthen cooperation to fight terrorism, including through the exchange of best practices;

5. *Reaffirms* the primary responsibility of Member States to implement the Strategy, while further recognizing the need to enhance the important role that the United Nations, including the Counter-Terrorism Implementation Task Force, plays, in coordination with other international, regional and subregional organizations, as appropriate, in facilitating and promoting coordination and coherence in the implementation of the Strategy at the national, regional and global levels and in providing assistance, upon request by Member States, especially in the area of capacity-building;

6. *Encourages* civil society, including non-governmental organizations, to engage, as appropriate, in efforts to enhance the implementation of the Strategy, including through interaction with Member States and the United Nations system;

7. *Calls upon* the United Nations entities involved in supporting counter- terrorism efforts to continue to facilitate the promotion and protection of human rights and fundamental freedoms, as well as due process and the rule of law, while countering terrorism;

8. *Calls upon* States that have not done so to consider becoming parties in a timely manner to the existing international conventions and protocols against terrorism, and upon all States to make every effort to conclude a comprehensive convention on international terrorism, and recalls the commitments of Member States with regard to the implementation of General Assembly and Security Council resolutions relating to international terrorism;

9. *Notes with appreciation* the continued contribution of United Nations entities and subsidiary bodies of the Security Council to the Counter-Terrorism Implementation Task Force;

10. *Underlines*, in that regard, the importance of greater cooperation among United Nations entities and of the work of the Counter-Terrorism Implementation Task Force to ensure overall coordination and coherence in the counter-terrorism efforts of

the United Nations system, as well as the need to continue promoting transparency and to avoid duplication in their work;

11. *Reaffirms* the need for enhanced dialogue among the counter-terrorism officials of Member States to promote international, regional and subregional cooperation and wider dissemination of knowledge of the Strategy in order to counter terrorism, and in that regard recalls the role of the United Nations system, in particular the Counter-Terrorism Implementation Task Force, in promoting international cooperation and capacity-building as elements of the Strategy;

12. *Welcomes* the progress achieved towards finalizing the institutionalization of the Counter-Terrorism Implementation Task Force, in accordance with resolution 64/235;

13. *Calls for* the enhanced engagement of Member States with the work of the Counter-Terrorism Implementation Task Force;

14. *Encourages* the Counter-Terrorism Implementation Task Force to develop a comprehensive website in order to ensure that its work is made accessible to a wider audience;

15. *Requests* the secretariat of the Counter-Terrorism Implementation Task Force to interact with Member States, including by providing quarterly briefings and comprehensive reports on the current and future work of the Task Force, in order to ensure transparency and to enable Member States to assess the work being undertaken by the Task Force and provide policy guidance and feedback on Strategy implementation efforts;

16. *Requests* the Secretary-General to submit to the General Assembly at its sixty-sixth session, no later than April 2012, a report on progress made in the implementation of the Strategy, which could contain suggestions for its future implementation by the United Nations system, as well as on progress made in the implementation of the present resolution;

17. *Decides* to include in the provisional agenda of its sixty-sixth session the item entitled "The United Nations Global Counter-Terrorism Strategy" in order to undertake, by June 2012, an examination of the report of the Secretary-General requested in paragraph 16 above, as well as the implementation of the Strategy by Member States, and to consider updating the Strategy to respond to changes.

117th plenary meeting 8 September 2010

"Napoleon... duh!"
by Thomas White

Don't forget to visit us at
http://www.themuniversity.com

CHAPTER 9: The Art of Crisis

Don't take life too seriously. No one gets out alive.

There are *too many possibilities* in Crisis Committees for us to focus on "What to do if..." scenarios. This chapter is focused primarily upon some key situations that will directly affect your success in a crisis.

Crisis Committees form the upper echelon of Model UN. The rules about them are mysterious and secretive to newbies. The power of social intelligence in the room is magnified, the critics of your plans are skilled and strong, and the opponent to your left is a manipulator.

When faced with this sort of environment, your mastery of the basics is assumed. *Eye contact* is no longer suggested, it is required. Your failure to extend social graces and exhibit a dominant *presence* will be treated with disdain. The chair will recognize immediately if you are a novice so the skills that we have described earlier become even more important. Though you may have won awards in larger committees, realize that the crisis committee is a new level of competition.

There are three branches to a Crisis Committee that are interacting with each other at various points during a conference: the Committee, the Chair, and the Crisis Staff. The Committee is at the whim of the Crisis Staff that acts much like a "choreographer" for the ever changing situation that needs to be resolved. Every decision your Committee makes will have some effect on the Crisis Staff who are deciding the direction of the conflict. This may sound confusing now but with more experience this dynamic will make perfect sense. Below we provide an example of an evolving conflict.

Example: The Evolution of a Crisis Committee

(US National Security Council, 2014, Egypt in Disarray)

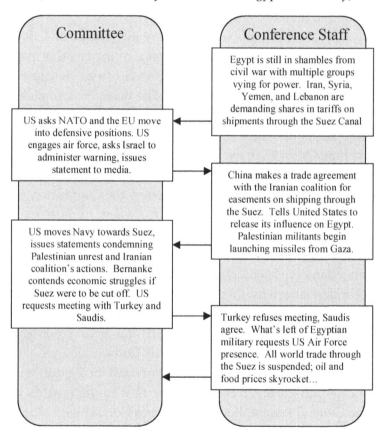

Committee	Conference Staff
	Egypt is still in shambles from civil war with multiple groups vying for power. Iran, Syria, Yemen, and Lebanon are demanding shares in tariffs on shipments through the Suez Canal
US asks NATO and the EU move into defensive positions. US engages air force, asks Israel to administer warning, issues statement to media.	
	China makes a trade agreement with the Iranian coalition for easements on shipping through the Suez. Tells United States to release its influence on Egypt. Palestinian militants begin launching missiles from Gaza.
US moves Navy towards Suez, issues statements condemning Palestinian unrest and Iranian coalition's actions. Bernanke contends economic struggles if Suez were to be cut off. US requests meeting with Turkey and Saudis.	
	Turkey refuses meeting, Saudis agree. What's left of Egyptian military requests US Air Force presence. All world trade through the Suez is suspended; oil and food prices skyrocket...

This chart shows a potential flow of events. Like in chess, the Crisis Staff must respond to your every move. If you can cause changes that the Crisis Staff was not expecting, you'll be a creative force that pushes them to acknowledge your innovative decisions. In large committees, your ideas and decisions are being sculpted over multiple days of committee sessions. In Crisis Committees, your ideas and decisions are ever **evolving** during a live simulation. The committee may cooperate with your vision, or frustrate your every intention. This fluctuation may occur instantaneously.

Every delegate who has run the gamut of Crisis Committees can share their experience of a crisis that was not administered well. In a room with fifteen delegates, there is a huge burden on the staff. The delegates can make very powerful decisions that could potentially steer the entire situation into a new direction. Imagine if the Egyptian Crisis that we used as an example earlier had suddenly broken into World War III. Chaos would ensue in the room leading to poor decisions by the Committee.

Most conferences do not weigh crises any differently than large General Assemblies. When considering the increase in difficulty yet the proportionately smaller size of the field of competition, we can understand why there's no difference in the weight of a gavel as it contributes to team awards. While we think it is a good idea to spread the field and give your best delegates a chance to grow into Crisis Committees, we also understand the desire to win; your best delegates will typically have a much better chance of winning awards in large General Assemblies than in Crisis Committees.

Any veteran delegate will try to explain the difficulties experienced during a Crisis Committee. As we said, these session are unpredictable so we can't instruct you exactly what to do, however, we have listed several ways that crises are more difficult than large assemblies:

1. There are very few rules.

   This means: *Crises are a series of directives and intel (essentially: directives are 'orders given' and intel is 'received information'). Therefore, people can be kidnapped and assassinated. Even you.*

2. There is more freedom for executive decision.

   This means: *Policy is not as strict. You can communicate classified information to the enemy if you want. You can release fake news. You can declare martial law. Taking risks is encouraged.*

3. The usual goal is as simple as maintaining security and stability.

   This means: *The word "crisis" implies an emergency. Emergencies need to be managed quickly, efficiently, and decisively. Imagine that a flu pandemic emerges and is spreading throughout the world. You're the CDC. Fix it.*

4. The biggest problems haven't even happened yet.

   This means: *Conferences usually choreograph long plotlines with several major events in succession. The events that happen may have nothing to do with your actions, or they may heavily depend upon how you and your committee respond. The staff may want to engage you, challenge you, or even aggravate you.*

The contents of this chapter are the game changers. Each section carves out a concept that you must understand in order to succeed in a crisis committee. These ideas and concepts are NOT very useful in a large committee for reasons that will be very apparent as you read. It's worth noting a few recent Crisis Committees. Many will begin with a highly specific goal in mind while others will exist amid events that cannot be controlled in the slightest. Let's examine some examples of titles that can be seen at conferences and make some *predictions* about the content of the committee:

MSUMUN's JFK 1964-1968 – This committee will undoubtedly concern itself with the stability of a country after the assassination of the president. Any member of this committee better research every single aspect of LBJ's presidency. Foreign relations, domestic fiscal issues, and the fallout of the Cuban Missile Crisis will all play a role in this scenario.

BOSMUN's Somalia 2011 – This committee probably seeks to establish a stable government and a self-sufficient economy... what else can Somalia hope for? The Somalian Navy (*We mean "Pirates!"*) and militant Islam will certainly factor into this mess of a weekend. Don't expect results.

ILMUNC's Napoleonic Wars – This sounds like a panel of Napoleon's chief advisors as he asserted his dominance over Europe. Some members are thought to have committed acts of treason...

certainly those events would play out. Don't be surprised if people are routinely executed.

CMUNC's Crisis at Kashmir – A long time ago (1940's) India became a sovereign state and religion has always been a big deal throughout the country. In the northwestern region known as Kashmir, generations of Muslims and Hindus have been very militant about their homeland (which goes back thousands of years) and the way that laws have been interpreted and administered therein. They still have issues. Cooperation amongst the multiple tribes of Hindus and Muslims would have to happen publicly... and a consensus of tribal lords would have to be appeased. Good luck there. Estimate thousands of casualties and assume there will be extended failures of compromise since it will undoubtedly concern the legislation of a consensus morality based on religion in a religiously adamant, yet intricately diverse region.

With the facts given, predictions could be made, but there will be surprises!

We hope this small list shows that there will be some predictable content, but the end result could take some dramatic turns. Imagine the way the following events would sculpt the respective committees we just listed:

JFK 1964-1968: What if the financial stresses of Medicare, education funding, and the human rights/desegregation movement prevented the invasion of Vietnam?

<u>Somalia 2011</u>: Imagine that an overseas multi-billionaire financier decides to invest in the protection of Somalian waters while demanding a low fixed price on tuna. How did this affect the economy of the region?

<u>Napoleonic Wars</u>: Is it out of the question that an advisor of Napoleon's may have convinced him **not** to enter Russia and he, instead, more deeply invades the Ottoman Empire?

<u>Crisis at Kashmir</u>: What if a new religious leader with messianic tendencies forms a third religious faction in the region? He unites the Hindus and Muslims of the area into a new religion reminiscent of Jainism, forming a third faction that local fundamentalists seek to obliterate. How would India and Pakistan deal is this issue?

You would probably not be prepared enough to effectively react to these situations regardless of your extensive research. They are completely hypothetical! There aren't any books written about events that did NOT happen. **You have to "fly blind!"**

This chapter centers upon the qualities that make a great Crisis delegate. There are a great variety of formats and procedures so we will not spend any more time on the logistics. We'll tell you what qualities will make you successful in a Crisis Committee.

We'll briefly discuss three major topics:
1. *Creativity and Vision*

147

2. *Writing*
3. *Your Frame*
   a. *Every delegate in a crisis committee is important.*
   b. *Adaptability is more valuable than a strong position.*
   c. *Consensus isn't based on an ultimate goal, but rather a journey.*

Creativity & Vision

These crises are geared to cause your committee to react. With every directive you write, you're sending it directly to a staff that has thought about this crisis for several months. When you think of an idea that they *did not think of,* that's when you get their attention. This *creativity* is the **biggest** ingredient to a crisis gavel.

You must do some brainstorming before your conference.
1. Imagine all of the people from your committee in one room. Imagine their hidden agendas. What might they try?
2. Imagine your character's own hidden agenda. Can you accomplish it?
3. What would be the ideal "historical" accomplishment for your committee? What is preventing that <u>historic</u> development?
4. Can you magnify and/or exacerbate a major conflict?
5. Are there any important people or political bodies that are not part of your committee but have a direct influence on the crisis?

You should ask yourself ALL of these questions before you begin the conference. You should research the answers to ALL of these questions and have them in mind when you begin. Strategy is extremely important.

Your vision of the *possibilities* is what will best prepare you for a crisis. Exploit all of your powers. Test the extent of your powers. Speak your mind and push for your plans but always keep a few tricks in your back pocket... just in case.

Writing

Your communication with the outside world is extremely important in a Crisis Committee. The most important requests for action are called **directives** or **action orders**. They are your specific requests for exact actions to be undertaken. You can move your armies, raise interest rates, request a face-to-face conversation with an opposing general (this is called a *personal communiqué* and is better used than a committee communiqué), you can even move spies, or bomb a city. Of course, all of these depend on your committee. If you're in a specialized agency like the Olympic Committee, none of these are possible. But if you're on the UN Security Council, all of these are open to you, if not by action then by request.

When you write your directives, you must be as clear and *specific* as a good resolution is. For example, you may put in a directive to "move troops to Iran." The staff may choose to move troops from a strategic position in Iraq to a not-so-strategic position on the northeast border of Turkmenistan and Iran. If you wanted a Navy Seals team to be available in Tehran, you need to specifically request to "activate 2 Seals teams. They are to be dropped in the Alborz protected area to the immediate Northwest of Tehran to allow for a two day advance to the Mehrabad International Airport where we are expecting

Ahmadinejad to be arriving in three days." Please notice the difference between the last two quoted directives. One is childish, the other sounds like a legitimate directive that we might read about in a presidential military briefing. Depending on the conference for your crisis, there is a small detail you need for your directives. **If you write a directive that you mean to keep confidential, you must call it a "Portfolio Order."** This establishes a *virtual* cloak of secrecy. However if the staff chooses they can claim, "the CIA intercepted your directive." (*This can happen if another member of your committee has already issued a directive to monitor your activity and tap your emails and phones*). This situation may happen rarely but we need to educate you of these possibilities.

The general format of a directive is as follows:

Portfolio Order
Author: Lieutenant ...
Signatories: (If you have any... you don't need any for personal communiqués)
   1. *Move troops ...*
       a. *Troops located ... will be moved to ...*
       b. *Strategy is to ...*
       c. *...*
   2. *Issue a request to meet with the ambassador of ...*
       a. *Intentions are to ...*
       b. *...etc, etc...*

One more detail that can keep you active when you feel you haven't written any directives for awhile: send out press releases. You can release true information or false information depending on your goal. If you've ever watched a detective show, the police will occasionally release false details about a murder in order to aggravate the assailant. This can be especially useful and manipulative when there is a deep egotistical dysfunction in the suspect. You can enable some of these tactics in committee.

Your Frame

This final piece of the chapter is meant to address your psychological state of being in a Crisis Committee. When an actor enters a scene, they put themselves in a mindset that we can call a "Frame." The three aspects being suggested here are chosen specifically because they are so different from your mindset in a large committee.

A. Every delegate in a crisis committee is important...
(but YOU must be the most important.)

You might think that this is obvious. We already know why your reaction is flawed. In a large assembly, you're thinking about the idea of "one man = one vote" and the process of democracy. You're thinking about convincing every *single* person to believe in *your* idea (*reread* Chapter 5: Rhetoric and Dialectic *for the finer details*).

In a Crisis Committee, your ideas will never gain the sort of traction that you're expecting in a General Assembly. Random events will occur and your entire committee will immediately have to shift their focus onto a new policy, or a different action... It can feel as if there's NO TIME! Strategically choose your allies and "plant seeds" with them. If you did your job and brainstormed for the potential futures that would erupt in this crisis, these people will turn to you when your predictions come true. Then you can let those "seeds" grow into fruition.

Believe in your powers of observation. Even if they are slightly flawed, your belief in them can overshadow the flaws... especially in a small room of teenagers. Yes, everyone is important and you should treat them as such. But you must believe that your ideas are the most useful and strategic concepts in the room. You are the "mastermind."

B. Adaptability is more powerful than a strong position
(but if you have predicted well, your position will be the strongest.)

The staff will always lean towards the "surprise" and "frustration" intent. You must expect that. A **CRISIS**—*again*—implies that there is an emergency, a major catastrophe, a calamity; there is a huge PROBLEM. This should be obvious. But you have to treat it with poise and show that you're masterminding the solution. There is a path to enlightenment... and you've got to be able to adapt to the stream of events that will attempt to frustrate your lofty goals. This is a game of chess.

Brainstorming and presenting a creative agenda are the lights to guide you through the three-day foray of a crisis. When a midnight crisis occurs, you'll have to present an immediate response that will be incredibly impromptu. The tests of adaptability are at their worst when decisions are required spontaneously and without any delay.

If you put the time into brainstorming about the problem, you're bound to have a few accurate predictions. You can propose these to the delegates you recognize as the most viable characters in the plot. Your vision can be shown as superior when your predictions come true. If you have gone the extra mile and prepared a few ideas for what to do if your predictions come true, then your position will be a commanding and impressive presence.

C. Consensus isn't based on an ultimate goal, but rather a journey
(and this journey would've never existed without your map.)

In large committees, the goal is for the room to pass your resolution. In a crisis committee, the goals are for the crisis to be accepted, "converted," and to prepare the future to proceed in a stable environment. Again, we understand your nervousness when it comes to these committees. There is an ever-present atmosphere of tension and anxiety because every single second counts.

Consensus, though a simple process in large assemblies, is a much different and quicker process within crises. When the events are chaotic, the proposed solutions can be just as chaotic as the events. The room will typically not agree until a series of solutions are adopted, just like when two working papers have merged to form a resolution in which multiple clauses are so similar that they must be combined and refined, while the entire resolution becomes a more "inclusive" *re*-solution for the problem.

When you brainstorm, you make a map. There are several possibilities that may emerge and your foresight can instigate the debate and negotiation that form the basis of those most decisive moments in a crisis. When you are already presenting the "Umbrella Ideas"(see chapter 5) before anyone votes on the details, you'll be seen as a virtual creator of the future. These suggestions may sound awkward but remember, Model UN is just a fantasy anyway. Your predictions can be the Manifest Destiny you've predicted, believed, and then declared. Let everyone else vote on the details. Just show them that you've already seen **the map.**

Now that you've read the only published pages on Crisis Committees, you're fully prepared to subject yourself to the teachings of the Dark Arts. Since the complexity of the room of delegates has been introduced in glorious detail, it will be no big deal for us to say that the upcoming information should be used carefully.

"Dark Forces"
by Thomas White

CHAPTER 10: The Dark Arts

An ye harm none, do what thou wilt…

You may have noticed that throughout this guide we have tried to remain diplomatic. We have shown you how to dress properly, speak properly, and think diplomatically to obtain success. What we haven't told you is that there are times during committee when you may have to get your hands dirty. You may even have to kill someone... FIGURATIVELY.

To quote the description of this chapter from our introduction: *"If you truly want to be at the top of the mountain, it's easy to see that there's much less room at the top than there is at the bottom."* The tactics of your opponents will get more ruthless as you ascend the mountain. The mountain is a powerful metaphor for you to embrace. People who stand just below you may attempt to remove your legs; you must be **aware** of them and everyone else too.

We will only give you a layout of the gray areas. The *Dark Arts* are called "Dark Arts" because great techniques exist which can be exploited for selfish purposes. We personally ask you to stay in the light... don't go evil. You may not be able to get back through the rabbit hole if you stray too far.

The Contents of this Chapter Include:
1. *A Recipe for Madness*
2. *The Cookbook*
3. *Advanced Rapport*

A RECIPE FOR MADNESS

Like an accomplished chef, you must include many different ingredients when making a meal. Learning how to navigate gray areas requires you to include every spice on the rack. Prepare yourself mentally. You are about to enter this rabbit hole known as the gray area. This is a place where rules do not always apply. While lost in this turbulent world you may ask yourself:

What do I do without rules?!

Answer: Rules aren't real; they are a manifestation of our social world. If men were angels there would be no need for government.

What kind of rules can I break?!?!

Answer: What would you do in a world with no rules? What would you do with all of that freedom? Model UN has simple rules that you already know and complicated rules that we've listed in the appendix that are called "parliamentary procedure." These rules are essential for directing debate and maintaining order. One example of a VERY strict rule is the restriction against pre-written resolutions. It's a good rule and you should follow it, but don't be fooled into believing that there are no delegates who write their resolutions weeks before the conference.

We have seen students with pre-written resolutions in our own experiences as Model UN advisors. You would be shocked at the extent they are willing to go to hide them from us before a conference. We do not allow that behavior, but we can surmise that where there's smoke, there is fire, and that other students around the nation are breaking this rule as well.

The rules we are discussing here aren't going to be this clear cut. Most of them will be *social rules which are much more flexible and not so well defined.* For example, men should wear pants, but what if your friend was supposed to be Julius Caesar in a historical crisis committee and he decided to wear traditional Roman garb for the first day of committee to show his creativity?

Although he has broken a "social *rule,*" this daring risk has helped to endear him to the chair. This can give "Julius Caesar" a huge advantage when the time comes to hand out the final awards due to his social intelligence. This simple example is the first Dark Art within the Cookbook: Peacocking.

So be careful. Use these tricks at your own risk. If you are not careful you may become a target for your opponents. Most schools frequent the same conferences year after year. You don't want to be remembered for using dirty tactics. They will warn their friends and you will get blacklisted.

THE COOKBOOK

Let's start simple. We want you to ease into these techniques, so let's start with the simplest way to attract attention: your look.

Peacocking
(as mentioned in Chapter 6... with added flavor)

Look at this picture:

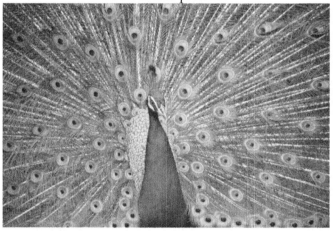

It is completely insane that evolution would have created a bird which can only be described as something so inexplicably extravagant. Do you know how this pattern of feathers evolved? It is simpler than you might think: female peacocks found this design more attractive than other *"less decorated"* males. In our culture, women usually "peacock" more than men, but many of your male classmates that spike their hair, wear colorful or gaudy jewelry, strap on big boots, and sport t-shirts with risqué designs are *peacocking*, too.

With the rules of attire that we've already set forth in Chapter 6, we'll now add some real flair.

Men:

Do something "daring" with your hair. Frost it. Spike it. Ponytail if it's longer. Look through a magazine like *Rolling Stone* and come up with an idea.

Wear a colorful button-down, maybe something as bold as purple. Wear a tie that is mature and nice but matches the color of the shirt. If your shirt is a boring color, make the tie super flashy and follow it by removing your jacket and draping it over your shoulder when you make a major speech.

Wear a few rings. Two on one hand and one on the other is plenty. If you have an earring, wear that too. If you have a nose-ring, you're already "peacocked." You can probably skip ahead since you've already accomplished the effect we're discussing.

The nation that you are representing may have some sort of cultural regalia that you can use to your advantage. Maybe you know of a store nearby that sells costumes or cultural clothes similar to your country's expected attire. If it slips over your clothes, put it on just as you're about to make your first speech. If you've already gotten over your self-consciousness, let everyone watch you put it on as you're about to speak.

Come up with something else that suits you. Don't be too crazy; remember that the rules should only be broken in moderation.

Note: *Don't combine too many of these suggestions. Two is plenty… Three is pushing it.*

161

Women:

Wear a pattern that is stylish but "busy." It will catch people's eyes. Wear shoes that *clomp* on the floor when you walk *normally*. **Don't *try* and make noise. The shoes do all the work.** Again, don't go nuts with the height of the shoes. More than three inches will make people wonder why you would torture yourself with that sort of discomfort; you'll attract the *wrong* type of attention.

Patterned stockings will also attract the wrong type of attention. Instead, wear a colored pair of stockings that stylishly match your outfit. Wear colorful or sparkling jewelry that is not expensive. Long cheap necklaces that go down to your waist can be conspicuous and slightly "clinky" but not annoying. Do your hair and wear makeup. Don't overdo it. Eyeliner, lip gloss, and **a little** rouge can go miles.

<u>**Note:**</u> *You can combine all of these suggestions. Women have fewer rules than men when it comes to peacocking.*

The Opener

You never get a second chance for first impressions. With a good first impression, you will make people smile and they will welcome you with open arms. The Opener is your spark to a conversation. Try one of these effective strategies to ignite a conversation you have with someone today.

Creating a Social Aura:

Creating the proper atmosphere is essential in setting up the Opener. There are two small pieces of information that you must know and practice all of the time in order to use this tactic successfully:

1. Keep a *slight* smile.
2. Act like you are **already** cool and comfortable with every new friend you meet. Imagine that they're old friends if that helps you accomplish your goal.

The slight smile is the first important element to your social aura because smiles are contagious. When you walk into a conversation with a very slight but very genuine smile, people can feel that you're happy. You will project an image that you have good intentions to the committee.

If you seem mean, weird, or too nice, it will be hard for people to trust you. You can't build a consensus if you can't hold the trust and esteem of the other delegates. Show an optimistic and friendly smile. People will *automatically* feel comfortable with you and you may win an instant alliance with a simple smile.

The second element to creating a successful social aura is to act friendly with the other delegates without appearing over eager or not genuine. Many people find it hard to strike the proper balance during their first interaction with a delegate in their committee.

Use a trick that actors use as a guide to establishing this rapport. Every time an actor takes on a role, they need to "frame" themselves mentally into the situation that they are going to represent. When you take on a "frame" you are creating your own 'picture' (*or more like a 'situation'*). The beauty of meeting someone new is that you can be whoever you want to be. If you act in that role and 'frame' the situation as if you truly are this person's close friend, they will usually play along.

Now that you've got these two behaviors to incorporate into each opener, we'll give you some basic lines to try.

IMPORTANT: These are not hypothetical examples. You are to USE these!!! Try them! Think of them like "training wheels." Sometimes we feel weird saying something that someone else told us to say. We may feel 'fake' when we make a joke that isn't really ours. Ignore these feelings. It's totally OK if the person you talk to doesn't know that it's not your joke. Only by using these examples of "lines" or "jokes" will you start to learn what interests random people.

DOUBLY IMPORTANT: If you just take these examples and use too many of them, you might come off as being too much of a joker and not serious enough. These are called **openers** for a reason. **Use them *sparingly* to START CONVERSATIONS with *new friends*.** Start them laughing, but the dialogue should become more earnest, interesting, and challenging as the conversation gets deeper.

Try and use these openers with as many random people as you can during a conference. Conferences have thousands of students. You should make a goal to meet at least 50 *new friends* in the course of your weekend. When you become a master of the opener, you should meet one hundred people over the entire span of the conference without even trying.

164

Examples of Openers:

There are two things that every human being finds interesting, relationships and mysteries.

1. Feel free to ask somebody their opinion about the relationship between two people, two countries, two celebrities, or maybe even a relationship question about a friend and her boyfriend.

2. Ask a random question about something that no one knows... for example:

   a. "Why are Russians called cosmonauts and Americans called astronauts?"

   b. "Should you floss before or after you brush your teeth?"

   c. "Why is everyone so entertained with vampires lately?"

   d. "Does that fur around your coat's hood really keep your face warm?"

Model UN provides a huge assortment of situational observations that you can share with a fellow delegate.

1. Is anybody dressed really inappropriately or really weird? When there's a dull moment in committee, make a joke about that outfit to the *new friend* next to you. Then laugh about it together until the next speaker finishes their speech. In a patient, relaxed and natural way, now ask them what sort of plan they're working on. Begin working your rhetorical skills from Chapter 5 and get them to start thinking about your plan instead.

Examples Of Jokes About Attire:
a. "Did that girl skin a cheetah to make that dress/pocketbook/bag?"
b. "Those two guys are wearing the same exact clothes! Ya think they woke up together?"
c. "Is the chair trying to look like [insert ugly celebrity here]?"
d. "Do you think God should smite people with faux hawks?" *(This is a perfect example of how* peacocking *can backfire)*
e. "He looks like his mom dressed him."
f. "I think she etched a mural in her stockings... or maybe she wrapped grandma's tablecloth around her legs... What do you think?"

2. How about some candid talk about countries? There's a ton of material that you could come up with to start chatting with your fellow "worldly" delegates. For example:
a. "Do you think Germans tip when they eat in Greece?"
b. "I think China needs more people. They should consider relaxing their border restrictions."
c. "When will Russia just give up? Seriously... nobody likes communism, you crazy red country. And you have too much land. It's just plain arrogance."
d. "Norway has good teachers. But, do they have school in igloos? How cold is it there? You think they have smarter polar bears, too? Who would've thought they'd have to deal with gun control..." *(that last sentence was serious, remember... start funny but don't stay funny. The more dimensions you can have in your personality, the more people will listen.)*
e. "How did Brazil get the Amazon, rain forests, Portuguese, ethanol, soccer, and Adriana Lima? It's so unfair."

f.   "Does Africa have light bulbs?"
g.   "You think that kid really is from [insert their country here]?"

3.   When unmoderated caucus begins, you have to be much more tactful with your entrances and exits. The openers have to be used with much better timing and you have to use more body language skills. Also, people form into large groups that are completely independent, each having a social life of its own. There is not as much freedom to be focused on one individual person... and there are MUCH fewer dull moments. *Opening* an entire group is difficult and not for the faint of heart. The following examples are obviously large group openers.
     a.   "HUDDLE!" Say this if you know that your group is going to form near you. If you use this shout well (like a call to arms), it can be its own form of "public-announcement-peacocking." People will know that it's you and they will always know where your group is meeting. (AND, you'll make it 'seem' as if you're the leader)
     b.   "Gavel, gavel, gavel! Tap, tap, tap! Decorum! Decorum!" Say it like you're the chair. Shout it at a decent volume but not like an obnoxious idiot. Warning: You better follow this shout with a good point.
     c.   Wait for a moment of conflict between the two loudest people who are trying to talk over each other. Look around the group and find at least two people that are really eager to speak and say something. With **authority**, say "Guys, guys! You both have valid points but can we calm down for a second cause [he/she/they] had a good point and if we can just listen for like 10 seconds, I think it can

167

help." Now point to one of those people. And then you can follow that person's speech by pointing to the next person. If you pull it off with good body language, vocal technique, and **assertiveness** (without being a bully) you can become the leader of the group... people will look to you to designate the next speaker... and even to finally put forth your own opinion since you've shown that you're such a good mediator.

d. As soon as the group of delegates is formed and you're near the middle, start with a *false time constraint*. For example, "Before we start, I just wanna say something... it'll only take 15 seconds!" Then hurry up and speak your opinion. So you've just told everyone that you'll be quick. This will make them feel like you won't hog the spotlight because you've already said that you'll only talk for 15 seconds. Even if you take 25 seconds, no one will count. Just don't repeat this multiple times... people will know that you're a liar. Also, this is a great one to use after you're already known as the "Huddle!" delegate.

e. The Clipboard Opener. Walk into the circle with a clipboard and a pen and tell them that you'll start jotting down each person's ideas. Pick the first person to tell you their idea, then move onto the next person. Summarize the ideas to the group and take ownership of the beginnings of the upcoming working paper you've just begun.

f. This last one is evil. Use only in an emergency. Tell the person who is obviously leading the group that you were just talking to the chair. Tell that delegate that the chair wanted to "ask a specific question" about their working paper. The group is now yours. Say what you need to say and get out of there.

168

These openers are all more useful than you can imagine. They will give you a "window" through which you can begin to build rapport. Most people are very shy and bashful and they would rather avoid conversations than begin them. You have to become the type of person that would rather BEGIN conversations.

Once you pick three or four of these openers and practice with them you'll get a better sense of what works and what doesn't. Your attitude almost **always** sells the opener so act appropriately during the delivery. After a very short time, you'll start to feel more confident and effective using these openers. Eventually, you'll even be able to create your own. You know you're really good at openers when you can pull off an improvisational version of this skill at the beginning of a committee session.

Advanced Rapport
AWARENESS, Part II

Welcome to the Matrix. Let's begin your training. All of the body language habits that you learned in Chapter 3 can be used to read your opponents. In this section body language, vocal technique, and rapport are going to be tied into awareness. From here on, we are going to assume that you have experienced some success, as well as failure, using the drills and techniques in this book. If you are sure you've spent enough time developing these skills then continue on to the next page. Don't be afraid to try and couple your observations with an opener as shown in the upcoming examples.

1. Do they seem stiff and too tight? Tell them to relax.
2. Are they smiling? Smile with them and make them laugh with a good opener.
3. Do they seem anxious or nervous? Reassure them that they're doing a good job, or that you're impressed by their ideas. Tell them they had a good speech.
4. Is somebody facing you and being very strong with their eye contact and body language? Is this a challenge of your ideas, or are you being socially challenged? If your ideas are being challenged, you must calmly stand your ground, question that person's assertions and demand proof of those opinions. If you're being challenged socially, smile and lean back. Tell them with a slightly placating tone, "I admire your 'fire.' It almost gives me chills."
5. Watch one group get together during an unmoderated caucus. Watch for two types of delegates. One type is the delegate who is trying to put his or her self right in the middle, be the loudest, and even *try* to be the best listener. The other type is the delegate who thinks it looks good to stand nearby the first type we just explained, but instead is obviously shy, uncertain, and would probably enjoy doing something else. If you want to add signatories and sponsors, choose the sheep. If you want to pick a person to argue with (so that you can attract attention), pick the first type, e.g. the assertive kid who's trying to get in the middle of everything.
6. When someone crosses their arms in a defensive posture, calmly fold your hands and listen to them.

Wait for someone else to react to that person then agree with the person who reacted and disagree with the defensive person. Whenever someone gets defensive, they're done negotiating and compromising. Eliminate that person as fast as possible.

7. When someone is relaxed and cool and you want to chat with that person, you must act more relaxed than they are. Don't stand, lean. Don't lean, sit. Don't sit, slouch. Obviously, do it all in moderation.

These tricks are almost their own category of opener. They can be used all day, every day. Work them into every aspect of your MUN game.

All of the vocal techniques you have learned need to be adjusted by your awareness of the audience. When you speak, be sure to monitor the audience and their reaction to your words. They will give you clues to how well you are speaking.

When people nod in agreement, don't change your message. Repeat your general idea and look for more people who agree with your argument. Try to maintain strong eye contact with those individuals who are really listening. Keep that eye contact while you're telling everyone in the room that you'll work with them on this issue.

As soon as you hear someone laugh at one of your openers, smile at that person and follow with your next line. Then ask everyone a question, a serious one or a random one, it really doesn't matter. Let them all talk about the question and **wait patiently** for the right moment to praise their thoughts. After they all have reported out their ideas, allow them the honor of hearing your opinion on the issue.

Watch for the person you're talking to keep eye contact and face you. If that person starts to look away and turn away from you, end the conversation and turn away from them, too. If that person keeps eye contact, faces you, nods and smiles interactively, make sure you keep the conversation going. Ask them a question.

If someone new walks in and stands near your group's conversation, open your shoulders towards them and attempt to shift backward to "open a door" for that new person to enter the group. Don't stand in a way that seems to exclude more people from entering the conversation. Open up your body's frame so that it looks like you are welcoming new people into your audience.

Conference rooms are usually tilted like an amphitheater. When you speak, try and take the elevated position when you speak. When you're addressing the entire conference room, make sure you lift your head and voice for the people in the back as well as the people right in front of you.

The audience gives you cues to use more opportunities to say your openers. Read the faces and body language of the people who are listening so that you can detect the rhythm needed to get MORE people listening.

Rapport is built after you've "opened" the group, demonstrated your value as a leader, and listened to how you can help them realize their goals. Once you are in rapport with a particular person or group, *staying* in rapport requires a bit of respectful attention, but not much else.

Final Options
...not for the faint of heart
We will not describe these strategies in this book because we do not approve of them, but we do need to make you aware of these techniques since they could potentially be used against you. Please take the opportunity to discuss these methods with more experienced delegates who have been in compromising situations or have used them before. Tread lightly.

1. Motion to table a topic.
2. Wiretapping and Waterboarding (in Crises).
3. Demand a roll call.
4. Motion to appeal the decision of the chair.
5. Motion to censor.
6. Incite opposition to your opponent.
7. Buy roses... (*of course we included this lame tactic*)

In Conclusion:
Most of the techniques in this chapter are used to meet people, be social while communicating your goals clearly, and then to stay in constant communication with them afterwards. Nearly every technique and skill can be adapted for real life situations from college interviews to chatting with grandma. When you begin to recognize the power of communicating with the right frame of mind, with skill and goal-oriented intentions, you will be well on your way to becoming a true diplomat. It will also become very clear to you who is socially intelligent and who is not. Believe us... the best Model UN delegates will be making the exact same observations.

"Not So Stick Anymore"
by Thomas White

CHAPTER 11: Going Digital
Follow/Friend/Like/Share/Search/Post/Verb/Verb/Verb...

The internet has changed the world!!! A programmable underbelly of creativity, communication, business, or decadence; it depends on who you ask. One thing is for sure, it will slowly permeate every aspect of our experience. To prepare you for the future, we wanted to include a special addendum that is (*sadly*) **not** being taught in American schools. As a matter of fact, there are multiple important skills that are not taught in American schools. The most notable exclusions from the curriculum are the laws that apply to you and your property, how banking works, first aid and natural medicine, and now computer technology. Yes, in most schools there are electives you can *option* to take that will teach you some basics about these topics, but in order for us to function as informed citizens we must learn a great deal on our own or elsewhere. Making "smart" voting decisions about the policies of our leaders is of paramount importance to any nation's future. Similarly, we thought you should know how to use the internet for **your future and career**.

The Internet Is The Future

University of Chicago's Chicago International Model United Nations (CIMUN) made a big splash in early 2013. They used streaming media to integrate their committees and creative an interactive conference experience. If the Security Council imposed sanctions on Syria, the US National Security Council might initiate a directive to monitor Syria's borders while the UN High

Commissioner on Refugees sends aid to nearby countries to assist with the refugees that will certainly be fleeing the economic hardships. This is how it works in real life. This is the interactivity that is coming to a Model UN conference near you. In the near future, we predict that conferences will begin recreating their small press and media communications committees, using journalism and digital media that integrates the posts of a centralized committee like the G8 or Security Council, and then that information would filter down into smaller committees as well as the GAs and ECOSOCs. The debate would become more dynamic. The delegates would feel tied into their fellow national reps in other committees, and the whole process would become a shared experience of an international, interconnected, global world.

A smaller, simpler vision of a digitally friendly

 This is a QR Code. You can scan it with any free QR Code App on your smartphone.

This one will take you to our facebook page.

accessory to the Model UN landscape might be the creation of a website or webpage that displays your delegation's position or *vision*. There might be links to each of your position papers that you can print as a QR code onto a note and pass to another delegate. It's a nerdy thing to do at the moment, but that sort of exchange is coming.

Outside of Model UN, you can be using these webpages as an organizer for your club. A QR Code can go on your school poster and take your classmates to a signup page. You can post a calendar for your club's important information, permission forms, school websites, research documents, position paper archive, and helpful links like

176

http://www.themuniversity.com!! Wordpress can do all of these things.

Another reason you should learn how to mess around with this kind of nerdy computer stuff, well, did you notice how many teenage millionaires just popped up out of nowhere? Read about Christian Owens from Corby, Northamptonshire in the UK who started a site where you can buy bundles of paid iPhone apps at a time at a fraction of the price. You can also read about Nick D'Aloisio who just sold his "Summly" app to Yahoo. We are not claiming that this is easy to do, but it *is* easier than you think. To be one of these software developers is a tall order, but you can have your own Wordpress website, connect it to your Facebook account, and/or connect those two things to your Twitter account with less than twenty minutes of simple clicks and texting in a few words like your email address and the name of your website. All three of these services are totally free. There are many, many others out there, but we've been using this setup for a year now and it is pretty simple. If you are interested in a different platform, you can use websites by Joomla or Drupal instead of Wordpress. Tumblr and the drag-and-drop sites like Wix or Weebly are nice and simple, but they offer much less functionality. In our setup, Wordpress will use a built-in plugin to tell Facebook and Twitter to post on your behalf.

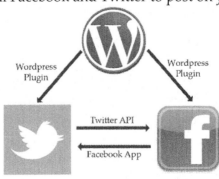

There is the option to have your own domain, email, hosting, etc. If you want to have your own "web hosting," you will have to pay for it. Wordpress can be your hosting service for free. You can also shop around and go to a website like GoDaddy.com or Bluehost.com where you can buy a domain (*FYI: most school or non-profit organizations use a '.org' address*) and allow their servers to host your files. There are nearly one hundred web service providers so choose wisely. Wordpress forces you to use its software (which is not a bad thing), but other web service companies allow you the choice to add Wordpress or other web software right onto your domain with a few clicks. Services usually include free email at your own domain, payment solutions, photo or media software, and much more.

Creating Your Wordpress Site

Creating a free wordpress site is much cheaper because it is free (*you will actually get more functionality "out of the box" with a free wordpress account because your wordpress site helps wordpress grow*). With an email address, you can sign up and create a domain, use free software for creating and managing your website, link your social media accounts (Twitter, Facebook, Tumblr, and LinkedIn), and follow other blogs. After a little practice you'll be creating pages quickly, linking to other websites, uploading photos, and you can even change the design of your entire site with a few clicks (*they're called "themes"; look at other websites that we've designed using Wordpress, ModelUNEducation.com and TheMUNIVERSITY.com, to see how different each can look, Best Delegate is also a Wordpress site*).

So let's just start this process. Before you start, open your browser and log into your Facebook, Twitter, and your email (this will make the process go much quicker once you're finally logged into Wordpress). Don't close your browser after you have signed in to those accounts. Open a new window and begin following our instructions on the very next page!

1. Go to Wordpress.com

Notice the little icons and the video. Feel free to watch it. It's informative and highlights the spectrum of possibilities that you can accomplish with Wordpress. Notice that Wordpress.com is also the place to log in to your Wordpress account once you've got your website up and running.

2. Click on "Get Started"

This next page will require you to complete the signup with your email address, a username, password, domain name, and it will offer you a series of "upgrades" if you would like to pay for them. We've taken the liberty of showing you our signup information.

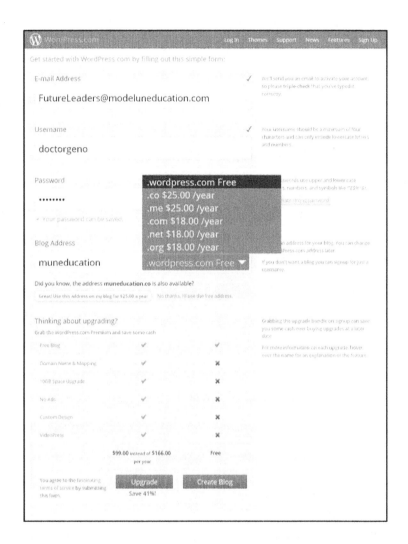

The blog address will be the link you give to your website (notice that our Wordpress site can be accessed at muneducation.wordpress.com). If you want to remove the ".wordpress." part of the address you're creating here, you'll have to buy your own domain name with the highlighted box. These prices are a little more expensive than the hosting websites we've already mentioned on the

180

previous page. Notice that if you create a free wordpress blog you'll have less storage space and wordpress can run ads. It's a small price to pay, but just fine to get started. There is much more to configure if you try and handle everything with another web hosting service, but if you pay Wordpress the $18/year for a dot com address the configuration is just as easy.

3. Activate from your email

4. Create the blog and pick a style

You can give your site a title which will be visible on the browser and in the blog, put a little tagline or subtitle right next to that title and choose your language. When you click "Next Step," you'll

be brought to a page that lets you choose a style or "theme" for your site. In my opinion, this is the best feature of wordpress. You can completely change the look of your website at the touch of a button. Later, when

you've got the hang of the look and feel of your site, you can go back to the dashboard (we'll show you what that is soon) and change your theme through the menu titled "Appearance→Themes".

5. Preview your style and start a post!

Wordpress will now give you a sneak peak of your new site and offer you the chance to make some customized changes. Feel free to try that or to get started with your first blog post which can be  accomplished with the very next step. You can post a video, a picture, or just a simple paragraph. If you'd like to

share another site, click on the "link" option. If you begin sharing your media files with your site, we **strongly** suggest that you create a directory on your home computer to keep copies of every file you share on your site. You will keep coming back to that directory over and over again as you think about your web content. If you begin reading about web design, you're going to see the word "content" written everywhere. Every single post of text or media is lumped into a big concept called **CONTENT** (*content is the new god of the internet, no joke*). If you keep your content fresh, interesting, and diverse, you can build a very popular site very quickly. As you begin putting content into your site, you'll also be changing your mind about how to present it. You might change your main menu buttons, categories, tags, and even the little links on your sidebars, etc. It may not feel organized and presentable for a few weeks and that is OK. Just get started now so that you understand the process. Remember, nearly all businesses, organizations, and events will have a website. Shouldn't you be familiar with the process of making and managing one?

6. Make a quick page and publish it

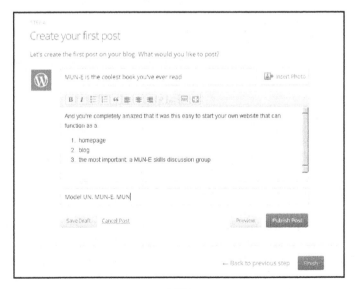

Wordpress already has a link button: 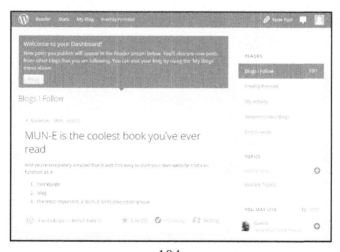 when you highlight some text, this button will form that text into a link. This is a tool for putting in a link to another website (called a "hyperlink"). You should use hyperlinks as often as possible! Search engines like google use the connections between websites to determine how to rank your site in a search. Hyperlinks are a big part of this. If you can manage it, <u>try to get other websites to link to your website</u>. Your site will move up in the search rankings **much** faster when other sites link to you. Your links are part of the ranking, too, but much less important than the links that connect **to** your website. There is also a set of formatting buttons, a box for tags (just like hashtags), a button for inserting photos, and much more.

7. Now find your dashboard and start using your site

The words "Welcome to your Dashboard!" come up on the next page that wordpress sends you to after you press "Publish Post" or "Finish."

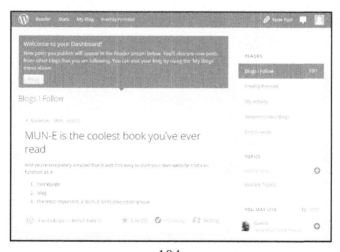

This is not the site-managing-*dashboard* for your site but instead it is something more akin to your Facebook homepage. The dashboard for your blog is two clicks away. On the first dashboard page, click on your post and it will take you to your blog.

Notice, because you are now signed in to Wordpress, the dark gray control bar across the top shows that you have been recognized as the owner of this website. In the top left, the title of your site contains a drop down menu that includes the REAL "**Dashboard**." This is where you really control the nuances of your Wordpress website. Click on the "Dashboard" button to go there.

What you're looking at now, is the modern world of website management. From this interface (*multiple other site managing software installations have very similar interfaces for controlling your site*) you can post, manage pictures, insert a logo, manage visitors' comments, create a group of users and administrators, and connect to multiple other services. If you've got a few moments, you should click on every single button along the left just to see what's "under the hood."

This Dashboard is where we're also going to connect your Facebook and Twitter accounts.

8. Click on Settings → Sharing

If you haven't connected to your personal accounts yet, do it now. Click on "Add new [your service] connection." Follow the simple directions by allowing the connection. When it's all done you can choose to share your new posts with those services. It's a great way to make one announcement and get everything updated at one time.

9. Add your own share buttons

It's always a good policy (*for site ranking*) to allow visitors to share your pages or posts. When you scroll down the Sharing page, you can drag and drop your share buttons right onto the Enabled Services bar. These share buttons will be added automatically to every post and page on your site. The convenience is just *magnificent*.

When people share your site, your search ranking goes up. If you upload lots of photos, you should have a Pinterest button. If you're hoping to make it a professional career site, you should have your LinkedIn account connected to your site.

Now make another post so that you become familiar with the process and how easy it is.

Plan your site for your MUN Club

This is a very specific set of suggested buttons and configurations for a Model UN club's website. We're giving this out of love; from the depths of our hearts, we do not want you to travel down the roads of despair that come from questioning your buttons and format. "How do I present all of the things I foresee myself sharing and posting?" is a question that you will ask yourself multiple times as your redesign the organization of your site as it gets bigger and more informative.

Your club needs to be a place where you can post membership forms, school waivers and nurse's forms for travel if you are a traveling club. These PDF or Microsoft Office files should be posted onto a Wordpress Page (not a

Wordpress Post) and titled "Forms." You can make that webpage a button that will appear under the main menu. For very important information like this, it should be very easy for your members to find. Make sure you and your officers are in agreement about the most important things that should be quickly available on your site.

You should have a Calendar available. Under your little user image in the top right of the dark gray control bar, click on the Help & Support button and search for "Upcoming Events Calendar." The top two pages in the search results will give you directions on including a google calendar or an iCalendar into a Post or a Page on Wordpress. Wordpress has a beautiful little set of commands that you can type right into your posts and it will run a little computer code called a "shortcode." Shortcodes can do all sorts of useful things. The shortcode `[upcomingeventsurl="ICALENDARFEEDURL"]` will insert a full interactive calendar. When you follow the directions and create a google calendar or an iCal calendar for your club, follow the directions to get the iCalendar Feed URL and replace ICALENDARFEEDURL with that url address. Wordpress will automatically insert it into the published page. We suggest doing this on another Wordpress Page and making it a menu button.

You should already have an "About" Wordpress Page that is in the menu. Click on Pages and click on it to edit it. Write a great description of your school, your club, your club's history, your awards and competitions, as well as your goals and most important events. Another nice Wordpress Page to put in the menu is a succinct description of what Model UN is. This is the most difficult page to write because you want to use this page to attract new members. The other problem is that Model UN is very

189

difficult to describe. Feel free to use some of our text to describe it to interested students. In this page you should also provide a nice organization of links to the UN, links to other NGOs, UNA-USA, to Best Delegate, to Model UN Education, and maybe even provide a good list of influential or powerful people who have participated in Model UN as students. These are methods for advertising.

Lastly, you should have a "Resources" Wordpress Page (again, with a button in the menu). This page will have links like cia.gov, conference sites, major international news pages, and pages about Model UN or even negotiation strategies. Create a booklist on Amazon and link to that. Link to your school's website (for good politics), your Facebook page, anything you want.

These should be enough to create a very good skeletal version of an organized MUN club website. Now you're MUN-E.

General Web Strategy

Having been working with Wordpress for a few years now, we would like to give you a little guidance and general philosophies about managing your website.

- Large fonts aren't a bad idea
- Make sure your colors are simple and contrast well
- Don't build a user signup until your content is legit
- Don't advertise until others compliment it
- Plan for posting at least once each week
- Add videos... try and make them GOOD videos
- Don't post like a maniac
- Do NOT post opinions without GOOD research

APPENDIX A
Guide to Parliamentary Procedure
The Flow of Debate, followed by the Compendium of Common Motions

New members of Model UN often have problems with the procedure and protocol that is associated with the conference. We've always found it helpful to think of Model United Conferences as if it were a complex dance. If you ever seen the TV show "So You Think that You Can Dance" then you probably have a good idea what we're talking about. In Model UN simulations the delegates are the dancers moving gracefully around the floor while the Secretariat is the choreographer who is trying to lead their dancers to its ultimate vision. The chairs are the three judges who score the event and many times, like the show, you may not agree with their scoring but you are forced to accept it.

The choreography for the dance is what a MUNner would refer to as the "Flow of Debate." The flow of debate is the order in which events take place during a Model UN conference. Much like a dance, debate will reveal itself at different portions of the simulation but at no point should you ever really stop moving. If you can understand the flow of debate and the due process associated with the simulation you have a distinct advantage over other delegates.

PROTOCOL

1. ROLL CALL

The Chairperson will take attendance at the beginning of a Committee session. After the delegate hears their country they should respond "present."

2. SETTING THE AGENDA

Model UN committees often use more than one topic. When this occurs the body as a whole must set the agenda by deciding which topic to work on first. At this time a delegate normally will make a motion, stating "The country of Eritrea moves to place _(Topic A)_ as the first topic on the agenda, followed by _(Topic B)_." Once the motion has been made, three delegations must speak in favor of the motion, and three other delegations will speak against it. Usually the speeches alternate between those in favor and those opposed. Following these speeches a vote is taken. Setting the agenda requires a simple majority vote.

3. DEBATE(*Treat each column individually*)

FORMAL DEBATE	INFORMAL DEBATE
Formal debate revolves around a speakers list. The Chair begins by asking all delegates who are willing to speak to raise their placards to be placed on the speakers list. The Chair then randomly selects delegates creating an order for future speakers. A country may only be on the speakers list once, but delegates may add their country to the end of	There are two modes of informal debate involving discussions outside of the speakers list: **Moderated Caucus** – the chair calls on delegates one-by-one so that individuals can address the committee in short speeches. **Unmoderated Caucus** – the

the list at anytime if they are not on it.

The Progression of the Debate

1. When the debate begins, speeches focus on stating a countries position and offering recommendations for action. (*Think of a trailer when a movie is first being advertised.*)
2. After blocs have met speeches focus on stating bloc positions to the entire body.
3. Delegates must now make statements describing their draft resolutions to the committee.
4. Delegates try to garner more support through formal speeches and invite others to offer their ideas.
5. Delegates make statements supporting or disagreeing with specific draft resolutions.
6. Delegates present any amendments they have created.

committee breaks for a temporary recess so that delegates may meet each other and discuss their ideas informally.

The Progression of the Debate

1. After several countries have stated their position on a specific issue, the committee breaks for caucuses in order to develop regional positions.
2. Writing begins as countries work together to create a draft resolution or working papers.
3. Countries and groups begin to promote their ideas in the committee. It is important to try and gather support for specific draft resolutions.
4. Delegates finalize draft resolutions.
5. Draft-resolution sponsors try and garner greater support for their resolution through mergers and friendly amendments. Much of this is accomplished behind the scenes during the informal debate.

4. CLOSE OF DEBATE

There are two situations that allow a committee to close debate. The first is when the speakers list on a topic is completely exhausted. In that situation the committee automatically proceeds to voting. The second situation is when a delegate feels that his or her country's position is clear to others and that there are enough draft resolutions

193

on the floor; he or she may make a motion to proceed into voting procedure by moving for the closure of debate.

5. VOTING PROCEDURES

Once a motion to close debate is approved, the committee moves into voting procedures. Voting procedures are closed to all outsiders. Only members of the committee are allowed to remain in the room and if you have the misfortune of getting caught outside of the room when the motion is made it is possible that you may be locked out of the room.

Amendments are voted on first, then resolutions. A delegation can vote one of three ways. It can either vote YES, NO, or ABSTAIN. If a country abstains it does not participate in the vote. Once all of the resolutions are voted on, the committee moves to the next topic on the agenda.

The Compendium of Common Motions

BASIC RULES AND PROCEDURES	REQUIRED TO PASS MOTION
A motion to set the speakers time sets or changes the amount of time each delegate has to speak	**Simple Majority Vote**
A motion to open the speakers list allows delegates to sign up to speak. At some conferences a motion to close the speakers list closes the list for the remainder of the session or topic. This motion is uncommon though, and most Model UN conferences will allow the speakers list to be open and closed numerous times throughout the debate. These types of motions require immediate votes.	**Simple Majority Vote**
Delegates can also propose a motion to suspend debate for the purpose of holding a caucus. If you move to suspend the meeting, be sure to specify the purpose and the amount of time.	**Simple Majority Vote**
A motion to adjourn meeting ends the committee session until the next session. The next session can be after lunch, after dinner, or next year. It all depends on the conference you attend.	**Simple Majority Vote**
A motion to adjourn debate (TABLE DEBATE) is not the same motion to adjourn the meeting. When you table debate you stop all work on a particular committee topic. Some conferences allow you to revisit the topic later. Other conferences permanently end all work on the topic for the remainder of the conference.	**2/3rd's Majority Vote**
A delegate makes a motion to close debate in order to move the committee to a vote, usually when the delegate has made his or her country's position clear and there are enough draft resolutions on the floor.	**2/3rd's Majority Vote**

A point of order is used when a delegate believes that the chair has made an error in running the committee. Use this with caution because if you accuse the Chair of making a procedural error and you are wrong it will be a painful mistake. The Delegate can only specify the errors they believe were made during formal committee procedure. Delegates should not address the topic being discussed at that time.	**Decision of Chairperson**
A point of inquiry (POINT OF PARLAMENTARY PROCEDURE) can be made when the floor is open in order to ask the chairperson a question regarding the rules of procedure. The floor is open when no other delegate is speaking.	**NO VOTE**
A delegate may raise a point of personal privilege in order to inform the chairperson of illness or physical discomfort that he or she is experiencing. It can be as simple as "I can't hear Portugal when they are speaking." or "it is too cold in the room."	**NO VOTE**
A delegate raises a point of information in order to pose a question to a speaker during formal debate. The speaker chooses whether or not to yield his or her time to points of information.	**Decision of the Speaker**
A delegate makes an appeal to the chair's decision when he or she feels the chairperson has incorrectly decided a point or motion. Very dangerous to use. Please exercise this appeal with care. Some conferences require that this formal challenge must be made in writing. The appealing delegate and the chairperson defends himself or herself before the vote.	**2/3rd's Majority Vote**

APPENDIX B
A Guide to Research
What to do and FAQ...

We did not include research as a chapter for one major reason: research is a simple process with very specific steps that should not need extensive discussion. There is no reason to write an entire chapter about research. You wanna know how to get good at research? *PRACTICE.*

Research never ends

Every time you do research, you are linking together the entire entangled web of information about human civilization, i.e. history, law, world affairs, international diplomacy, etc. Every single time you look up facts, you must interpret how those facts fit into the entire picture of human history. How do the events, laws, and interests of the executives of past provincial states influence the other events from that era? How does the situation from the background guide foreshadow the future events in history? How does your country represent the interests of the essential human pursuit of happiness?

We'll ask again: you wanna get really good at research? *PRACTICE.* Start piecing the world together today. Read a book. We'll suggest a few for you to start:

1. *The Next 100 Years: A Forecast for the 21ˢᵗ Century* by George Friedman
   a. This is a book on the ENTIRE modern geopolitical climate. Extremely informative for people who do not know very much about the

current state of affairs throughout the entire world.

2. *The Enemy at the Gate: Habsburgs, Ottomans, and the Battle for Europe* by Andrew Wheatcroft

   a. This book is about the struggle for power in Europe during the 1800's and is a remarkably informative foundation for understanding Europe's current political landscape.

3. *Genghis Khan and the Making of the Modern World* by Jack Weatherford

   a. As you can tell, these books are going back in time. This book is an amazing perspective on the details of the creation and operation of an empire.

4. *Military Geography: For Professionals and the Public* by John Collins

   a. This is an amazing book. It gives you an entirely new way of viewing the security (and expansion) of a country.

History and politics are a **big** deal. You need to appreciate the size and complexity of the stories that "**make**" history. Read one of these books... they're all very different though we recommend them in the above order due to their applicability to your MUN policies.

One BIG detail is that you need to read these and CARE about them. You need to be *interested* in these stories. If you aren't interested, you won't remember what you read and all of your investment in your research will be forgotten. (*If you don't care, then why in tarnation are you even reading this book?*)

NOW... follow these exact steps to do your research. We've created two separate outlines for "Present-day" and "historical" topics. Sorry, if you join the Harry Potter-themed "Ministry of Magic" committee, you're on your own... and we apologize for refusing to acknowledge your existence. Put your invisibility cloak back on.

RESEARCH STEPS FOR PRESENT-DAY COMMITTEES

Step 0: Read the background guide... duh. Research everything in the background guide that you don't know about. Start a small journal and write about how you feel about the details of this topic thus far. If you can establish an *emotional* connection to this content, you'll retain it much better.

Step 1: One or two months ahead of time, you need current information. Get a good magazine: *The Economist*. One comes out every week. Get it every week. Read *at least* a quarter of the whole magazine. A quarter is not much... but you'll quickly understand why I told you to read this magazine once you get started.

Step 2: Go to the CIA factbook – the website is given here:https://www.cia.gov/library/publications/the-world-factbook/
Read everything about your country and your country's neighbors. Who are your allies? Who does your country have a poor relationship with? If you are a person, go to wikipedia and start there (*if you want REAL references from wikipedia about a particular subject, pay attention to the little numbers that look like this "[9]"... click on them for the actual reference and see if you can find that reference on the internet*). Then ask yourself the same questions about allies and enemies. TAKE NOTES as you do this stuff!

Step 3: Based on the topic of committee, the current world's political pulse, and the major players in your community, choose a *motivation* and go check out the next appendix for help with the position paper. Write a draft of your position paper EARLY. You don't <u>need</u> to have the final draft done for a while... but you should still do it EARLY. When any project is nearly done, it becomes natural to keep your eyes open for more ideas! If you want proof of this, read ahead in one of your classes. In a few days, you'll notice that you understand the teacher much better than you did before.

Step 4: Concentrate on the current issues in the world that directly relate to your country's positions and "supposed" intentions. Start thinking about your potential arguments, compromises, strategies, and goals. Do it in that order. Write them down.

Step 5: Go find facts to prove your arguments. Go back to chapter 5, remind yourself of those concepts. Now with a friend explain the important issues in your committee, your delegation's place in it, and then have some practice arguments.

Step 6: (*Expert*) Go to the United Nations website and search for recent resolutions passed in your exact committee... or research trade and military agreements between your nation, the region, and larger organizations such as the NATO, OPEC, WHO, UNESCO, NAFTA, etc.

RESEARCH STEPS FOR HISTORICAL COMMITTEES

Step 0: Duh. Read the background guide. Research everything in the background guide that you don't know about.

Step 1: Find a book that tells the story about the historical events occurring at the time of your committee. READ IT. Trust us, there is a book about every major historical event... especially if it's in the 20th century. Get a book and read it EARLY.

Step 2: Talk to your history teacher about this issue. Your teacher will be more helpful than you can imagine. Ask questions! Go to wikipedia and start there (if you want REAL references from wikipedia about a particular subject, pay attention to the little numbers that look like this "[24]"... click on them for the actual reference and see if you can find that reference on the internet). Then ask yourself the same questions about allies and enemies. TAKE NOTES as you do this stuff!

Step 3: This part is hard. Think about the possibility of something different happening in the past... and how the future could've been different. What could your delegation do differently in order to change what actually happened in history? If you had your way, how could the situation have turned out better for those you are representing?

Step 4: Now write your position paper... EARLY. Get this done EARLY!!! Even if you didn't do all of the other steps yet...

Step 5: Go find facts to prove your arguments. Go back to chapter 5, remind yourself of those concepts. Now with a friend explain the important issues in your committee, your delegation's place in it, and then have some practice arguments with another person.

Step 6: (*Expert*) Study the resolutions passed in your exact committee if the UN existed at that time in history. Otherwise, research trade and military agreements between your nation, the region, and larger governments or organizations of the era. Study the details of these agreements!!! The minor details can be MAJOR turning points in committee.

We're done. It's really simple. Do as we tell you. The biggest problem that people have with research is that they just don't do it. They procrastinate and lack the attention span. Forget all the issues and stress. Just DO IT. READ. SEARCH. READ. SEARCH. WRITE. READ. WRITE. READ. SEARCH. READ. WRITE. ARGUE. READ. ARGUE. SEARCH. ARGUE…

…and suddenly, people will start to think that you're really smart.

FREQUENTLY ASKED QUESTIONS ABOUT RESEARCH

1. How important is the background guide?

It's very important. If the committee strays from the background guide, the chair may allow it. You have to be ready either way. The background guide gives you your **origin.** You have to start somewhere.

2. How much time should I spend on research?

Don't worry about time, just make sure you start EARLY. You need to train your mind to start "thinkin" about your committee's topics and issues. When you have already thought of questions, you'll be able to remember them in history class. You'll remember them when you're talking to a friend who knows about your topic. You'll be able to look up websites and read articles that are important to the topic.

3. I'm not representing a country. I'm actually a person for my committee. I don't know where to start!?

I'm a person, you're a person, and the kid next to you is a person! It's more natural to play the role of a person than a representative of a country, right? You need to imagine that you have a job to do and your entire reputation is on the line! You have an important role to play. Read about the person you are supposed to be. Try to find their biography and/or articles that have been written about this person's decisions. Search for the person on Google. Is there anyone who has written about them?

What did they do? What was their job? Who do they control? What is the most important thing this person has ever done? If you were them, what would you have done at that time in history? Did people like or hate that person?

4. *I don't know what to look for. I feel like I'm reading so much, but I don't get any better in committee! What should I look for?*

We understand this complaint. There's a huge mental block that many people have when they start their research. READ THIS CAREFULLY and REALLY THINK ABOUT IT. You have to research with the "frame of mind" that YOU are the person to solve the problems of the world. YOU have to establish a goal. YOU have to do your research as if YOU are the ONE person who really cares.

When people have this problem with research, they are always reading and searching as if they're in history class or English class. They read their references like they're reading a novel from class that they don't even care about. All of these situations and issues are the results of stories. If you're uninterested in the "story" of the world's events, you shouldn't bother with Model UN. LIVE IN THE STORY. Imagine that YOU are part of the story. You'll remember much more.

5. *What do I search for?*

Have you read the background guide? Start there. Grab a pen and circle every name, country, organization, acronym, fact, and event that you are not familiar with. Search for them as you go through the background guide. Every time you get to a point where you're confused, search for the issue on Google. Once you get a good feel for the scope of the background guide, you need to follow the rest of the steps from the above guidelines. After you go through the steps, keep searching for more pieces to the puzzle so that you become an expert. Look up the major players and read their biographies. Look up recent crises involving the countries in your local neighborhood. Study the CIA factbook and focus on the economy, the racial demographics, the government structure, major method of import and export, mortality rates, women's rights, the history of the largest cities, and the history of the politics of the entire region (was it part of the Ottoman empire, USSR, conquered by Germany in WW2, former territory of the UK.

6.   *How can I show my chair that I did this much research?*

If you did your research, it will be obvious to everyone in your committee. If you haven't done the research, that will be obvious, too. One tactic you can use to show your thorough research is to approach the chair early in committee (*or even before committee starts*) and ask about some *VERY SPECIFIC* **RECENT** world events that are directly related to the topics from the background guide. Ask whether the chair would allow for these recent events to be discussed in committee. You can also go so far as to tell the chair how useful a particular article or book was for understanding the background guide. Remember, the chair and her staff have spent WEEKS working on those guides. They enjoy being appreciated for it. If you bring up an interesting point, you will probably be picked for an early spot on the speakers list.

APPENDIX C
A Guide to Club Management
The Art of Wu-Wei/War for Advisors

The vernacular of this appendix will take on a strikingly different tone than the rest of this book. As teachers we must walk a tight line between allowing organic growth while limiting the potential for unintended calamity. Each of us has a very unique personality and our personalities are expressed through our interactions with our students. What is presented here is biased by our personal style. What you take from it will be biased by your personal style. Appendices are meant to be efficient, so we will do our best to keep to that motif.

Disclaimer

We are going to use the classic disclaimer, "the following guidelines are for novelty purposes only." Do not expect that our advice works in every situation. Do not assume that we have illustrated a legal framework for supervision. You do not have to adapt any fraction of our general philosophy to your own management protocols. This appendix is written for advisors who could use some insight. We have had numerous discussions with first-year advisors who are completely lost and confused about the process of Model UN. Some ask us "what should we do about [you fill in the blank]?" All we hope to do with this appendix is create a skeletal framework to help you help your club. Training may seem daunting at first, but eventually you will have a group of teenagers who are more experienced at this activity than you can everhope to be. These students will become your trainers. Your officers can run a smooth ship if you let them. Give them your faith. Model UN is about leadership. If you can't trust your officers to run the ship, what is the point of having a club that trains students to be leaders?

The Mind of the "Noob" Delegate

Our club's success has been the result of our trust in our members' ambitions. A majority of them have strong desires to be successful at this activity. We cultivate that desire. When they ask us for advice, we treat them as equals and assist them as if we were studying for the same test. Our belief is that we are helping them become leaders, whether in their committee or as a member of our club. If we wish to cultivate "leadership," we must allow them to lead. We cannot force their hand and make them a follower. We must allow them to make their own mistakes, lovingly point out those mistakes when they occur, and reverse engineer the situation using our social intelligence strategies and the common sense that comes with human nature.

Have you ever heard two of your students discussing their separate crisis strategies? We have very similar conversations with them about strategy but we take it up a notch and apply classroom management techniques. We talk to them as teammates, as if our mutual success is on the line.

Emotions can run wild in Model UN just as they can in any high intensity sport. Due to the "spotlight" nature of this activity, we believe that Model UN pushes on a more sensitive set of psychological buttons than most sports (*obviously **not** including gymnastics or wrestling or* *figure skating)*. It has been shown that public speaking is the most common fear of the general population. Our students are doing this throughout the day over multiple days. They are vulnerable to the judgment of their peers and this can be very unsettling to beginners (*"newbies"* or *"noobs"*). These students do need nurturing, but also a strong dose of matter-of-factness. After a few slightly discomforting reflections are bestowed upon them, they come to appreciate the *loving* honesty of our critique. To this effort, each student receives another disclaimer that is delivered differently, dependent on the disposition of the young soul we esteem with our guidance[†]:

> "Our criticism may feel personal because it is. Model UN is a very personal activity. You are using your body language and interpersonal skills with a bunch of adolescent strangers who are looking for every opportunity to judge you. We are helping you minimize the unhelpful social habits you have been programmed with. If it feels uncomfortable for you to make eye contact, we will point out your uncomfortable eye contact. If you have a distracting nervous tick like moving your arms too much or rubbing your hands together too often, we will tell you to keep your arms still as if we were your parents. We are NOT your parents, though. We are telling you **WHY** your peers will **respect** you more if you show poise. We are showing you that the entire room **responds better** when you make eye contact with the crowd. We will show you how to make small changes to your behavior that will yield *incredible* gains in rapport as well as respect among your peers. Human beings respond in predictable ways when you begin to experiment with the stimulus you give them to respond to. We are here to help. Accept our criticism as constructive and you might just evolve into a powerful, dynamic leader."

This conversation needs to happen very early in your relationship with the students. The type of criticism that makes students better at this activity can feel very personal

---

[†] This statement is somewhat satirical, though there is always a shred of truth in humor.

to them. They do not yet understand that body language and vocal tone are skills that can be honed and perfected. They think that the "cool" kids are born with this ability. They think that the great speakers are "super smart." They do not realize that they have the very same ability to become incredibly powerful personalities. We tell them that we will cultivate this power; we will help them evolve as a person. Their confidence in their own abilities is the key to every success they will attain, and that confidence is our focal point. Chapter 2 explains it all.

A Well-Oiled Machine

The club needs to operate autonomously to be at its most effective. Students (or more specifically, your officers) should not always be leaning on you for every decision they must make about meetings, training, committee assignments, choosing delegates who have earned the right to go to the most competitive conference, club fliers, and their email communications. The productivity of the club diminishes with every imputation of an unnecessary hierarchical approval. We suggest giving the officers the executive power to make all of the decisions we have just listed, give or take a few actions that satisfy your comfort level.

We have a president, vice president, treasurer, corresponding secretary, and recording secretary. Each of these positions comes from an end-of-the-year election with the officers for the upcoming year decided before the current school year ends. This overlap allows a smoother transition than can ever be accomplished by waiting for the following year. The Model UN calendar needs approval within the first week or two of our school year, and we would fail miserably to meet that deadline were it not for the two or three summer meetings we use to prepare for the season.

With five student officers, our club of more than 100 students runs smoothly. It seems to be a law of statistics that one of these five will "slack off" or become difficult to "track down," but one or two also rise to meet the challenge with enthusiasm. As teachers we each have our own limits as far as the behavior we will tolerate, but as this is a very social club that attracts some of the most intelligent and (*not always for good reasons*) "politically talented" students in the school, we believe that any student removed from their office needs to commit a relatively egregious "misstep." When they are failing to meet expectations, they should be reminded of their commitment. If they need reminding multiple times and/or have gone AWOL, they should be offered an opportunity to resign before being removed.

Officers need to be **present** in order for the club to operate with consistency. Attendance should be the officers' job. Training should be the officers' job. Simulations of debate should be run by the officers as well. A teacher/advisor should always be present or within earshot but not scrutinizing each and every action. Imparting some instruction is definitely called for at times of chaos, but an authoritative figure cannot be overzealous with their control when the subject of the lesson is LEADERSHIP.

On the other hand, when the students succeed, praise copiously. These students' confidence is crucial to the development of this club. They should feel successful in implementing their plans each week. They should feel accomplished when they make that thirty-second speech that the rest of the club responds to.

We suggest a weekly rundown that begins with a moderated discussion on current events.‡ Officers should be ready to give quick tutorials on any news that is unfamiliar to the general population of the club. Members should be encouraged to comment on these stories and potential policy decisions that may result. If a debate occurs, all the merrier. A well-moderated discussion of each week's world events should last at least twenty minutes.

At this point we suggest diving into your training. Officers can use some guidance at first, but generally they should be running the show. As veterans of the club, they should have a working knowledge of the typical exercises that have been practiced for the past few years. If your club is very fresh, choose some of the drills from the rest of this book and modify them for group activities. Common activities include moderating debates (*about ANYTHING*) where onlooking students can offer constructive criticism on tone, delivery, and persuasion (note the *disclaimer* from a few pages ago), reviewing a position paper and revising it as a group, splitting into small groups and being forced to come to a consensus on a particular international policy decision, or reading a report together and collectively brainstorming the research one should do to create an informed opinion. This is by no means an exhaustive list.

---

‡If your officers are not paying attention to national and international news headlines, you need to make it a requirement. This club **cannot** succeed without students who are "aware" of international debate topics.

Travel Arrangements

This section will be severely biased by our history of bus arrangements and public school budgets. Unlike most of the consistent MUN clubs out there, we hail from a public school. Our deadlines are extremely strict, our prices must be competitive, and our liability factor is open to a hierarchy of speculation. We will not discuss the nuances of airline booking because we have never done it. Our prices are capped at a psychological limit of $400. In November of every year, we plan a trip that books two full charter buses (85+ students and 8-10 chaperones), 28 hotel rooms for three nights, conference fees, and we usually target ~$275/student. For some traveling clubs, that price is a fraction of one airline ticket.

If you are in a similar boat, aim for three quotes from charter companies in the local area at least two months before the date of the trip. For hotels, the same time constraint applies. We have a philosophy on hotels: never stay in the hotel designated by the conference secretariat. On a long trip with a bus or two at our disposal, we subtract nearly all of the potential for "foreign club comingling" when we stay at the Midtown Hotel instead of the Boston Sheraton for HMUN (*we also save approximately $500 on one hotel room for three nights... multiply that by 5 or 6 rooms*). One "security update" at a conference's advisor meeting is enough to remind us of the consistency of our good decisions to keep our kids far from headquarters.

Since each student's cancellation usually accompanies a slight price hike for everyone else, you have two options: 1. Students must commit early and parents must sign a form that details a refund policy as the date

213

approaches[§], or 2. Price the trip at least 10% more than the final cost. Any surplus can go towards fundraising for future trips.

The skeleton of a typical itinerary goes as follows: our students report to homeroom on the first day of the conference. We minimize traffic by scheduling the bus to arrive after school buses have dropped off the general population. We board the bus and start a 4-7 hour journey. There is one stop for a 30-minute meal and bathroom break (there is a bathroom on the charter bus). Upon arrival at the hotel, students remain on the bus until advisors have managed the logistics with the front desk. Students are given an exact time to be ready in their western business attire. We check them in personally each time we transport the cargo. We assign a curfew that is strictly adhered to and all pizza deliveries are expected to arrive within +/- 15 minutes of that time limit. Infractions result in appointments with the "No Fun Zone." Note: when students get situated, keep a strict eye for connected rooms.

Our nighttime protocols might seem extreme to some, but the service staff at nearly every hotel we've stayed at have been extremely grateful for our management. At curfew we knock on every door, ask how the debate is going, detail the coming day's important check-in times, and we place masking tape on the door. Again, that may sound extreme but it helps us quickly manage our (*somewhat*) hourly nightly rounds.

Noise infractions can get students kicked out of hotels and we must thus rule with an iron fist. The "No

---

[§]Example: 100% refund at least 3 weeks ahead, 75% 2 weeks ahead, 50% 1 week ahead, 25% during that week, and no refund if the cancellation is the day before.

Fun Zone" consists of time intervals of utter boringness. A student will sit silently alone with nothing to do for at least an hour while a chaperone stays very closely nearby. There are ways to make it a bit more psychologically painful, but we'll let you be creative in your own administration of long distance discipline.

Over the course of a day of committee sessions, students must check-in with us, face-to-face, at a central location at least three times. Our usual check-ins are prior to boarding the bus for the morning, post-first session or prior to lunch break, post-second session or prior to dinner break, and post-final session prior to embarking for the hotel. Final check-in is at curfew.

In summary, despite the way we administer our protocols, you can do as you wish. Our intent is to be helpful. We are noticing that school trips are becoming a rare phenomenon and thus it becomes imperative that experienced teachers share their tested out-of-the-classroom management practices. It also seems that advising a school club is becoming more of a hazing procedure for green teachers, pressuring them to "earn their tenure." This implies high rates of "advisor turnover" and an increased potential for inexperience to result in poor student behavior, even dangerous behavior since they are so far from home. From one teacher to another, we understand the current state of the profession and sincerely appreciate your efforts. We are optimistic and hopeful that it will get better for all of us.

GLOSSARY

Terms in alphabetical order:

Absent Joe – This is the delegate who shows up to a conference with little to zero motivation for participating. They sit in the back of the room, play on their cell phones, and slouch.

Activist – This delegate truly appreciates Model UN and all of its ideology, and usually ends up shooting himself in the foot by being too nice.

Chair – The arbiter of the committee.

Charismatic confidence – The attitude of a winner.

Committee – A congregation of delegates participating in formal debate.

Compromise – Cooperation between delegates that support opposing positions.

Dialectic – A method of resolving disagreement through reason and analysis of arguments.

Delegates – People who represent the interests of a country or organization.

Delegation – A general term referring to a delegate or group of delegates representing one particular country or organization.

Diplomacy – The characterization of professional compromise between political organizations.

Diplomat – This student is the strongest speaker and team player. They constantly seek compromise and represent the ideals of Model UN with Teflon smooth sensibilities.

Economic and Social Council (ECOSOC) – The ECOSOC serves as the central committee for debate of international and social issues, formulating policy recommendations to members of UN.

Gavel Hunter – Beware of this delegate. He or she will seek to possess the gavel at all costs. Usually arrogant and overzealous, this delegate is still remarkably strong. Everyone notices this person.

General Assembly (GA) – The GA oversees the UN budget, appoints members to the Security Council, and makes policy recommendations to other parts of the UN.

Goal-oriented perspective – This is a frame of mind in which you formulate goals and align your actions to accomplish them, one at a time.

Humanitarian aid – This is a form of help given to people who are in need. This may come in the form of money, water, food, security, clean-up, medical assistance, or any other form of welfare promoting the general health of an ailing group of people.

Inflection – A vocal technique of using dynamic changes of volume and emotional stresses to make a statement or speech more understandable.

International Court of Justice (ICJ) – A group of international judges that interpret laws from multiple countries and international agencies in order to settle international legal disputes and advise on legal questions submitted by other UN organs and agencies.

International Delegate – The participant from a foreign school is usually an eager participant who tries very hard but is unsure how to demonstrate their confidence in the American social culture of insane teenagers.

Merge – When separate blocs, each promoting their own *very* similar resolutions, rewrite them into one comprehensive resolution.

Newbie – A student who is very new to Model UN. He or she can make mistakes very easily and usually has a very idealistic view of the motivations behind politics.

Rapport – A social bond or connection where two or more people "understand" each other.

Rhetoric – The art of using words to properly position an argument.

Security Council – A UN organ that is charged with maintenance of international peace and security.

Secretariat – A group of approximately 44,000 individuals operating under and with the Secretary General whose primary motivation is to carry out the decisions mandated by the principal organs of the UN.

Selfish – An adjective describing someone who acts only for him or herself.

Selfless – An adjective describing someone who acts for the welfare of others.

Speed/stop/slow down – A useful pneumonic device for remembering to pace yourself during speeches and in conversation.

Teflon Smooth Character – This is a metaphor for a person who seems very cool, no matter what situation they are in. The Teflon Smooth character exhibits body language and listening skills that make it immediately obvious that they are very socially intelligent.

United Nations Trusteeship Council – This council oversees the governance of former trust territories and mandates to assure that the inhabitants are administered according to their best interests.

Universal emotions – Feelings are universal phenomena and maybe very similar reactions to similar events across all cultures. They comprise the ideas of happiness, sadness, fear, security, pride, desire, anger, and love.

Veteran – This delegate is very experienced but still seeking the coveted gavel. Usually their failure is in the social game.

Volume – The loudness of your voice is very important for your public speaking. You must be aware of whether your listeners can hear you or if you are being too loud.

At Model UN Education,

Our Mission is to provide students with the skills and knowledge to succeed in a world dominated by an exciting, new process called globalization. At Model Un Education, we believe that excellence is achieved by a combination of social intelligence and academic intelligence, nurturing the perfect environment for successful, friendly and professional interaction. Model UN provides the platform that a student can use to practice this necessary, modern skill set. By understanding how to be social, diplomatic, and friendly, students who participate in MUN can eventually contribute more productively to a purposeful conversation as well as global, collaborative action. We are not revolutionaries, but "Evolutionaries!"

If you would like to order large sets of this book for your club or for a Model UN class, please email us at:

bookorders@muneducation.com

We offer discounted wholesale prices on bulk orders that can also be re-sold as a fundraiser for your club. Find us on Facebook at:
http://www.facebook.com/ModelUNEducation

and on Twitter: @MUN_Education

REFERENCES

[i] Truman, Harry S: "Address to the United Nations Conference in San Francisco," April 25, 1945. Online by Gerhard Peters & John T. Woolley, *The American Presidency Project.* http://www.presidency.ucsb.edu/ws/?pid=12391.

[ii] Sun Tzu translated & annotated by Ralph D. Sawyer (1994). *The Art of War.* Barnes & Noble. ISBN 1-56619-297-8.

[iii] Corley, M.; Stewart, O. W. (2008) "Hesitation Disfluencies in Spontaneous Speech: The Meaning of "Um." *Language and Linguistics Compass:* 589-602.

[iv] Jonathan L. Freedman & Scott C. Fraser. "Compliance without pressure: The Foot-in-the-Door Space Technique." *Journal of Personality and Social Psychology.* Vol 4(2), 195-202.

[v] Huang, M. S., & Byrne, B. (1978). Cognitive Style and Lateral Eye Movements. *British Journal of Psychology*, 69, 85-90.

[vi] Chartrand, T. L, &Bargh, J.A. (1999). The Chameleon Effect: The Perception – Behavior Link and Social Interaction. *Journal of Personality and Social Psychology,* 76, 893-910.

[vii] Fredriksson L. (1999). Modes of Relating in a Caring Conversation: A Research Synthisis on Presence, Touch, and Listening. *Journal of Advanced Nursing,* 30(5), 1167-1176.

[viii] DeCasper, A. J. & Fifer, W. P., Of Human Bonding: Newborns Prefer Their Mothers Voices. *Science, New Series,* Vol. 208, No. 4448, 1174-1176.

[ix] Amato P. R. &McInnes I. R. (1983). Affiliative Behavior in Diverse Environments: A Consideration of Pleasantness, Information Rate, and the Arousal-Eliciting Quality of Settings. *Basic and Applied Social Psychology*, Vol. 4 (2), 109-122.

[x] Kellerman, J., Lewis, J., & Laird, J. D. (1989). Looking and Loving: The Effects of Mutual Gaze on Feelings of Romantic Love. *Journal of Research in Personality,* 23, 145-161.

[xi] Ekman, P. & Friesen, W., Facial Action Coding System: A Technique for the Measurement of Facial Movement. *Consulting Psychologists Press,* Palo Alto, 1978.

[xii] Rosenthal, R. & Jacobson, L. (1968). *Pygmalion in the Classroom.* New York: Holt, Rinehart & Winston.

[xiii] Machiavelli, Niccolo (1961), *The Prince,* London: Penguin, ISBN 978-0-14-044915-0. Translated by George Bull.

[xiv] Collins English Dictionary - Complete & Unabridged 10th Edition 2009 © William Collins Sons & Co. Ltd. 1979, 1986 © HarperCollins Publishers 1998, 2000, 2003, 2005, 2006, 2007, 2009

^{xv}For a great example of how to write like a delegate check out the Council of Foreign Relations webpage. Under the "experts" menu you will find **Barack Obama's** link to his public statements about his policies. They are listed as you scroll down his page. It can be found here: http://www.cfr.org/experts/world/barack-obama/b11603
^{xvi}The United Nations was founded with goals that include the welfare of all nations. Your resolutions are expected to be a "collective" solution to a worldwide problem. Your resolutions need to be inclusive and you should acknowledge outside advice.
^{xvii}If you'd like to see the official format of a Model UN resolution, you need look no further than an actual UN resolution. Check out some General Assembly resolutions at
http://www.un.org/en/ga/63/resolutions.shtml

Made in the USA
Monee, IL
07 March 2021